THE LEADERSHIP FILES

*From around the world,
across a century*

THE LEADERSHIP FILES

From around the world, across a century

EDITED BY JULIA CAMERON

In association with

Evangelical Fellowship in the Anglican Communion

First published by Dictum in association with EFAC, 2020

Dictum Press, Oxford, UK
dictumpress.com

© For this collection: Dictum, Oxford
Sources listed on p111. Used with permission.

All rights reserved.

Scripture quotations taken from the New International Version. 1973, 1978, 1984 by International Bible Society

Foreword © Joni Eareckson Tada

If I am to lead
© Main text: OMF International omf.org
© Foreword to 1999 edition: Sinclair B Ferguson

Five marks of a Christian leader © Dictum

The leader as servant
© Main text: Ajith Fernando
©Foreword to 2006 edition: Lindsay Brown and Patrick Fung

Leaders who last © Vaughan Roberts / Lausanne Movement

Godly leadership in the workplace © Willy Kotiuga / Lausanne Movement

Leaders who ask big questions
© Main text: Elizabeth Catherwood
© Foreword to 2007 edition: Paul Batchelor

Ideas for reflection and discussion ©Dictum
The Art of Good Governance © Dictum

Design by Chris Gander

CONTENTS

Acknowledgments — vi
From the Editor — vii
Foreword by Joni Eareckson Tada — xi

PART I LEADERSHIP IN CHRISTIAN MINISTRY

If I am to lead – D E Hoste — 3
Five marks of Christian leadership – John Stott — 24
The leader as servant – Ajith Fernando — 36
Leaders who last – Vaughan Roberts — 62

PART II LEADERSHIP IN THE SECULAR WORKPLACE

Godly leadership in the workplace – Willy Kotiuga — 74
Leaders who ask big questions – Fred Catherwood — 84

Ideas for reflection and discussion — 107

Appendices

1. Sources — 111
2. The Art of Good Governance — 114

ACKNOWLEDGMENTS

The care of Phyllis Thompson in researching her biography of
D E Hoste, and including in it so much of his correspondence, led
directly to Alan Stibbs's work in producing in 1968 the oft-reprinted
booklet *If I am to Lead*. We are indebted, under God, to both of them
for their foresight.[1]

My thanks to Sue Brown for introducing me to *If I am to Lead* in
1981, and to Stephen Nichols and David Jackman in the 1990s
for encouraging its republication, leading in 1999 to the edition
published by OMF International. Fast forward to a conversation
in 2017 with Georgina Bartlett, then a postgrad student in Oxford.
Georgina had read the 1999 edition and suggested it be re-published
again for a new generation.

It was Las Newman, former Associate General Secretary of IFES,
who encouraged Sir Fred Catherwood to write, in 2007, *Light, Salt
and the World of Business*.[2] I'm grateful to Elizabeth Catherwood
for permission to re-publish much of it here; as I am to Ajith Fernando,
Willy Kotiuga and Vaughan Roberts for making their work available
again.

My thanks, too, to Rosemary Statter and Felicity Scullion, with
whom I worked closely in the Lausanne Movement, for help and
encouragement along the way with sections of the book then
published as Didasko Files; and to Jonathan Nimal, for tireless efforts
in getting those Didasko Files known in the IFES world.

JEMC

---

1. Phyllis Thompson (1906-2000), missionary in China, then Editor of
China's Millions. A prolific mission biographer, her writing always lucid
and well-researched. Obituaries: *The Independent; The Times; Evangelicals
Now*. Alan M Stibbs (1901-1971) also a missionary in China, later Vice
Principal of Oakhill Theological College; writer and editor whose work
played a significant role in the resurgence of British evangelicalism.

2. Here *Leaders who ask big questions*

FROM THE EDITOR

We hope you will find this collection helpful, whatever your leadership role. You may be a manager in business or industry, or lead a church, or a mission agency, or a student fellowship. Or perhaps you are a member of your church council, or you lead a midweek Bible study group.

The idea for this book grew out of a conversation over coffee with a student friend. I had earlier lent her my copy of Hoste (pp3-24), by then out of print. Sensing its unusual value, she asked if it could be made available again for a new generation of leaders. I was unsure whether people would read excerpts from letters to missionaries in China written a hundred years ago, but she felt they would. The content was clearly strong, and perhaps she was right. I recalled how much I had benefited from it as a young student worker.

From here came the question of what else might be given a new lease of life through a new publication. Books will last for decades, so it was better to bring a collection together in an unhurried way, and the selection took place gradually. While there is naturally overlap in areas covered, there is no repetition, as writers come in from different angles, and from different backgrounds.

In a digital age we too easily overlook the power of printed short books, which can get passed on, read on planes, then handed to leaders of ministries, or to publishers on other continents. Parts of this book have reached into many languages in this way.

A book in two parts?
While Part I relates specifically to spiritual ministry, and Part II to the secular workplace, this is not to suggest a sacred / secular divide. The biblical principles are the same in both contexts. And many leaders will move from the secular workplace into pastoral leadership in the course of the same day.

We hope you will find stimulus from the whole book, including the Appendix on good governance. Parts will relate to your own responsibilities; the rest will, we trust, help you in understanding the responsibilities of others.

Young entrepreneurs in your church or student fellowship may find particular inspiration from the stories in Fred Catherwood's chapter.

I'm grateful to Joni Eareckson Tada for kindly agreeing to write the Foreword. Joni founded Joni and Friends (*joniandfriends.org*), a formidable global ministry to enable people with disabilities, and she has led it for over forty years.[3] It has grown to incorporate online training and church resources, as well as giving practical help. Its 'Wheels for the World' campaign

---
3. Joni is a prolific author. Joni and Friends International Disability Center (JAF) works to change attitudes to people with disabilities. *Disability in Mission* Ed: David C Deuel and Nathan G John (Hendrickson Publishers with JAF / Lausanne, 2019) is causing radical reappraisal of how people with disabilities contribute to mission at all levels.

has, at time of publication, provided almost two hundred thousand wheelchairs for those in need, each accompanied by a Bible. Joni knows what it means to oversee, to recruit well, to delegate, and to be in it for the long haul.

Contact us through *dictumpress.com* if we can be of help – by giving a discount on bulk purchase, or making the book available to publishers or ministries in other countries, in English or for translation.

For those serving in churches or mission agencies: Pablo Martinez's *Take Care of Yourself: Survive and thrive in Christian Ministry* (also Dictum) acts as a companion title to this one.

Julia E M Cameron
Oxford, UK
June, 2020

FOREWORD

The book you hold in your hands is dangerous. If you hope to glean its insights, you must forget everything you have been taught about personal power leading to effective leadership. Confidence, charisma, and chutzpah count for little in God's Kingdom. I learned this the hard way.

Let me share a little of my story. Many would say that I am a key global leader in international disability concerns; however, I remember a time when I disliked every person I knew who had a disabling condition. From the militant activist who chained himself to a city bus, to the wheelchair students on my college campus who whined over every injustice. I disliked them all. The odd thing was, I was a wheelchair user, too.

My problem was with my own disability. I didn't like it. Being among others who had impairments only underscored my own weaknesses and frailties. That made things worse. My attitude started to change as I began spending more time in God's Word. I was stunned to see the degree to which Jesus loved those who were weak and frail, including the blind, the lame, and those who were paralyzed like me. I heard him whisper, 'Joni, these are the people I want you to serve. Lead them, just as I am leading you.' I did not like hearing that directive.

Yet the more time I spent in the Bible, the more I was impressed with the humility of Christ and his deep affection for the least, the last, and the lost. Especially those with disabilities. They followed him because they knew he cared. They followed him because he led with grace, humility, and wisdom. They followed him because he changed their lives. These became reasons I wanted to follow him too.

Jesus — the greatest leader who walked the earth — avoided the power brokers and the movers-and-shakers, to pour his energy and effort into the weak, the lame, the ill-equipped, unskilled and untrained. The surprising thing? These unlikely men and women became his greatest leaders.

This gave me a new perspective on my wheelchair. It also helped me see why God wanted me to serve him in the disability community. God takes great delight in deliberately choosing weak and unlikely candidates – such as I was – to get his work done. There can be no occasions for boasting. No hints of superiority. And no suggestions to those we lead that 'your opinion is not needed here'. When people acknowledge their limitations, God gives glorious and liberating freedom – freedom not to hog the spotlight, not to commandeer discussion, and not to insist on getting things your way. When people acknowledge their weakness, God releases them to *lead* in the best sense of the word.

Dan Allender, author of *Leading with a Limp*, has wisely said, 'The leaders God chooses are more broken than strong; more damaged than whole; and more troubled than secure.' God takes great joy in pouring his power, wisdom and understanding into people who truly rely on him. Thus, the most effective leaders do not rise to power *despite* their weakness; they lead with God-blessed power because *they recognize* their weakness.

How do we know when spiritual leaders are effective? They have followers who are passionate and committed. Like Jesus, these leaders effectively cast a vision— yet they feel no qualms about 'rolling their sleeves up' or getting down on their hands and knees to model the vision. Jesus cast a remarkable vision in Luke 14:13-14. 'When you give a luncheon or dinner, do not invite your friends, your brothers or relatives, or your rich neighbors... But when you give a banquet, invite the poor, the crippled.' No one better modeled that vision than Christ himself.

You will learn this style of leadership from the remarkable contributions in this book. *The Leadership Files* is a repository of sage guidance and tested principles. D E Hoste's wisdom has lain undiscovered by recent generations and I am delighted to see it made available again. John Stott and Ajith Fernando bear the unmistakable marks of humility and heartfelt service, and have long been recognized as key influencers in the global Kingdom of God. Vaughan Roberts, Willy Kotiuga, and Fred Catherwood provide deep leadership insights, as well, honed and shaped by their faith, convictions, and their unyielding passion to lead like Jesus.

THE LEADERSHIP FILES

I'm especially grateful to my friend Julia Cameron who has compiled and edited their timeless lessons. Julia has taken great pains to preserve enduring principles which will help all who long to grasp their Savior's gift for casting a vision, modeling it, and motivating followers who, in turn, will lead others. The Appendix on Governance holds much distilled wisdom for all who serve on Boards. Younger readers – remember it's here, as you may be called to take such responsibility in years to come.

I must say one more thing. Decades have passed since the days I was ashamed of my wheelchair. My love now is very great for people with disabilities, those I used to scorn when I was first injured. I answered the vision God gave me. As a result, he placed me on the National Council on Disability to contribute to the passage of the Americans With Disabilities Act. He also placed me on the US State Department's Disability Advisory Committee under Condoleezza Rice. He gave me the opportunity to serve with Lausanne as Senior Catalyst on Disability Concerns. And I still provide leadership to Joni and Friends, a ministry which serves the global disability community in the name of Christ. Your story will be different from mine, but for both of us, if we are willing, God will use us.

So, take a deep breath and get ready to flip the page of this dangerous book. Prepare yourself to learn a fresh, new way of bringing influence from a selected few of the Kingdom's most respected leaders. Get ready to cast God's vision, as well as to model it. And do not be ashamed of your brokenness and weakness – it is your pathway to leading with wholeness and in his strength.

Joni Eareckson Tada
Joni and Friends International Disability Center

PART I

LEADERSHIP IN CHRISTIAN MINISTRY

IF I AM TO LEAD

D E Hoste

Foreword to the 1999 Edition
(36 Steps to Christian Leadership)

The name of Dixon E Hoste is not well known today. But there are three reasons why he deserves to be better remembered.

The first is that he was the second General Director of the China Inland Mission (CIM), the chosen successor of Hudson Taylor. Hudson Taylor's name remains as well-known as his successor's is forgotten. Yet any man who can follow and advance the work done by such a pioneer and legendary figure must himself be an individual of outstanding stature. Dixon Hoste was such a man. Coming as he did from a regimented and highly-disciplined military life he brought the natural talents and spiritual graces which the Mission needed at such a strategic time in its history.

The second reason Hoste deserves to be remembered lies in the fact that, paradoxically, he lived to be forgotten. 'Live so as to be remembered' is stirring counsel. But there is another side to the fruit of God's grace: 'Live so that you will be forgotten, and Christ will be remembered.' That counsel may fuel devotion to Christ in many young hearts momentarily;

but to sustain it over the long haul is a challenge of major proportions. And it is here that Dixon Hoste serves us as such a model.

Even when he was a young missionary, people spoke of being 'impressed by his lowliness'. We tend to be drawn to the trappings of leadership; Hoste's leadership impressed people by the sheer force of his lowliness and humility. What appears to have struck so many people was not so much the power of his personality, but what Scripture calls 'the power of godliness'. We do well to listen to such a man.

There is a third reason why Hoste should be remembered. His gifts lay in his prayerfulness, his thoughtfulness, his wisdom, his passion for evangelism; in his thinking rather than in powers of speech.

HOSTE WAS A MAN WHO THOUGHT. HE WAS WISE

For D E Hoste was a man who thought. He was wise: 'If I have any gift at all, I feel it is along the lines of applying Christian principles to life.'

The statistics of the period of his directorship tell their own story of his faithfulness. Those years saw the Mission grow from 780 to 1,360 missionaries; from 364 organized churches to over 1,200; from 400 outstations to over 2,200; from 1,700 baptisms in a year to 7,500.

At a critical juncture in its history, the China Inland Mission had a wise head and a prayerful heart to lead it, and a steady hand on its rudder to guide it into the future. The pages that follow will give you glimpses of what that must have meant to the large numbers of Christians who looked to Hoste for counsel and encouragement.

This republication will bring D E Hoste's wisdom and style of leadership to younger men and women in whose hearts God has begun to stir up a desire to serve him without reservation. It is from among these that the leadership of Christ's church will come. The value of these pages is out of all proportion to their length. For my own part, I wish I'd had them long ago.

Sinclair B Ferguson
[Then] Minister, St George's-Tron Church, Glasgow

Excerpts from a few of D E Hoste's letters to missionaries during his leadership of the CIM (1900-1935). Some workers were in very isolated situations. His letters were always biblical and pastoral. ⟶

IF I AM TO LEAD

D E Hoste

An unsigned Foreword to the 1968 edition quotes Hudson Taylor as saying of Hoste's words that they 'ought to be written in letters of gold'. (Available in full at dictumpress.com). He was, as Sinclair Ferguson wrote in 1999, 'a man who thought. He was wise.'

SPIRITUAL LEADERSHIP

1. What are the marks of true Christian leadership? Let me suggest what to look for. If a Christian leader demands obedience on the strength of his position, he is acting like a tyrant. A spiritual person will approach things differently. He will want to influence the way others think. He will do this by handling them with tact and sympathy, drawing on spiritual power and sound wisdom by praying. He will not pre-judge things.

2. It isn't easy to keep an open mind until all the facts have been established, but we must do that when we need guidance in handling complex matters. I have often noticed that very gifted people find this difficult. In fact the ability to do it is quite rare. A leader has to

> *A LEADER HAS TO SUSPEND JUDGEMENT WHILE HE LISTENS*

suspend judgement while he listens to all that has to be said on a matter, and weighs it. In this way he will come to a sound conclusion, *and* carry with him those people who are affected by its outcome. They need to be confident in him, and in the rightness of his judgement.

3. I am sometimes asked what my most difficult job was as a General Director. I think it was to influence the way my most senior team members thought and acted. That was probably my most strategic task, too. To do it, a leader really needs to know he is 'speaking the very words of God' (1 Peter 4:11). This involves a holy fear and trembling before God, and a right attitude of heart to others. Unless a leader is truly wrestling with the powers of darkness, he will find himself wrestling with his co-workers. As Paul writes, 'The Lord's servant must not quarrel; instead he must be kind to everyone, able to teach, not resentful. Those who oppose him he must gently instruct...' (2 Timothy 2:24, 25).

On influencing the way people think: I have often been reminded of the Lord's teaching that it is hard to obtain 'bread' to feed others. We need to guard our own spiritual lives carefully if we want to pass on spiritual truths from Scripture, even truths which we may be struggling with ourselves. 'How painful are honest words!' (Job 6:25) and 'How good is a timely word' (Proverbs 6:23). But again, such words are not easy.

QUALITIES FOR LEADERSHIP

4. I believe the ability to appreciate a wide range of different people is the main quality for leadership. Each brings different gifts and abilities, and we need to help them all in different ways, depending on their personality.

I have learned from experience how vital it is to know people well, by observing them in a range of situations, and seeing how they relate to different people. For example, I remember once thinking how well a particular man would suit a role. But as time went on I realized he did not learn from others, and then weave what he had learned into his own thinking and way of life. History shows us that many of the great political and military leaders owed a lot to just this kind of learning.

5. As time goes on, I am persuaded more and more that the spiritual and moral qualities needed to handle church affairs and to guide other workers are found in people from all walks of life. Social background has no bearing on the matter. The clinch issue is that they are really men and women of prayer, who deeply distrust their own judgement and impulses, and who form views – and express their views – as they are taught and guided by the Holy Spirit.

SOCIAL BACKGROUND HAS NO BEARING

6. Those making policy decisions sometimes have to modify what they would like to do if it meets with a lot of opposition. These planned projects, or courses of action, may be very good ones in every way, but it is wiser to delay them if they are not approved by some people whom they affect.

I shall never forget the impression Hudson Taylor left on me in the way he handled such tricky situations. Frequently he either modified his plans or dropped them for the time being, as he judged that opposition was more harmful than leaving matters unchanged. Later on, after he had prayed patiently for a change of heart in those who opposed him, he was able to introduce the changes. This kind of patient, persevering prayer has played a more vital and practical part in the development of the work than most people have any idea of. We come back to that basic and holy truth - that the spiritual is the best practical.

PREPARING FOR LEADERSHIP
7. David was prepared by the suffering and danger he went through. Painful as it was, he needed to learn through this if he was to be saved from failing in the same ways Saul had failed. Those who want to be fruitful in their service of God can learn much from David's life. They must not be cast down if they find things going wrong, their plans coming to nothing, and even if they find themselves discredited by others and humiliated. That is just the time to 'humble

(ourselves) under the mighty hand of God' and, in the words of Psalm 131, to be as a weaned child before him. That is the only way to get rid of the self-will and self-energy which too easily become our masters when our lives are ill-disciplined.

8. If anyone feels too hemmed-in by their circumstances, or feels that life is not congenial enough, they should reflect on James's words, 'perseverance must finish its work' (James 1:4) or, as an older version had it, 'let patience have her perfect work'. By insisting on the kind of role which they feel they deserve, they may make it impossible for the God of Abraham to shape them for the service he wants them to give later on.

RELATING TO FELLOW-WORKERS
9. We all want to be used by God as a means of blessing. Our usefulness to him in this way can often be impeded by a bad relationship with someone else and we do well to be aware of this. Let's ask ourselves whether we would be more fruitful in God's service if we worked harder at getting on with another Christian, or another group of Christians. Are we prepared to make the first move in healing the division? We are commanded to lay aside ill-feelings, to confess our faults to one another, and to humble ourselves so such rifts can be healed.

10. From early in his ministry, the Lord Jesus was quite explicit to his disciples about the need to put right whatever they had done wrong to others as far as they could (see Matthew 5:23, 24). That is to say, God will not accept our service or our gifts if our relationship with fellow Christians is not right. So often I see spiritual dryness and unfruitful ministry which can be traced back to a matter in which this kind of teaching has been ignored.

> JESUS WAS EXPLICIT ABOUT THE NEED TO PUT RIGHT WHAT THEY HAD DONE WRONG

11. Sin of any kind grieves the Holy Spirit, but bitterness towards another child of God causes him special pain. In the same way, love and unity between Christians brings his special blessing.

12. If the Holy Spirit does not leave us, in spite of all the ways we grieve him, we should be very slow to say we cannot work with some other Christian. When we think of our own failings, and the frequency with which we make mistakes, it should make us gentle and patient with our fellow-believers. They may not have had the advantages we have had, or the opportunities to learn.

13. As the Lord called Abraham away from his home and all its comforts, we could have expected him to give Abraham a companion who was helpful and easy to get on with. But he didn't. In fact whilst Lot did have a measure of faith, he was weak, selfish and unspiritual, and more a cause of strain and anxiety than a source of strength and comfort. Abraham had to handle this relationship, and the trial and discipline it brought were God's means of forming his character and working in him those moral and spiritual qualities Abraham needed to be 'father of many nations'.

HOW TO GET THE BEST OUT OF PEOPLE

14. Think of the way the Lord Jesus handled his apostles, who formed the early church and in due course went on to plant churches in new places. It was by patiently bearing with them in their lack of insight, their unbelief, their pride, their hardness of heart, their instability and their other faults. He not only bore with them, but he entrusted them with his ministry and with a measure of his power, sending them out as his messengers to the Jews. Above all, he constantly prayed for them. Let's note, with reverence, the courage, the faith, and the hope he showed in the way he handled his disciples. These are vital qualities of a great leader.

Over and over again the Bible shows us people who seem unpromising at first, but develop into great servants of God through being trusted to bear burdens, face dangers, make decisions, and go through difficult times. True, they sometimes stumbled and fell under their trials. But as the proverb says: 'though a righteous man falls seven times, he rises again (Proverbs 24:16).

15. I'm sure the Church has lost people whom God could have used in his service because leaders didn't see their potential. Instead, they have been put off by faults and weaknesses which the people could have grown out of, given the right sympathetic influences and a sense of being valued.

> THE CHURCH HAS LOST PEOPLE WHOM GOD COULD HAVE USED

We too easily become stereotyped, narrow and critical in our judgement about others, especially the young and inexperienced, and in doing so we fail in a crucial area of leadership. A Chinese proverb says: 'The good ruler is able to make use of men'. In other words, he can perceive and find scope for the gifts of a range of people, taking into account their limitations. He recognizes that people with one particular area of gifting often lack other gifts. We need a *team* of people who bring different strengths. You cannot bore a hole with a good hammer, or drive home a nail with a saw!

SPEAKING AS IF FROM GOD

16. We can't discern God's mind for the way we should carry out his work unless we spend unhurried time in Bible study and in prayer, learning from him and listening to him. Spiritual power in our ministry, that is the power which shows people their need of Christ, and builds up Christians in their faith, comes only through the hard work of intercessory prayer.

I remember the effect it had on me when I began to understand the Lord's teaching on this. He said it would not be easy to know the right words to say to another person, or to a group of people, whether Christian or pagan.

God is no respecter of persons; the true worker for Christ who persists in prayer for 'bread' to feed others – whether fellow-workers, church members or unbelievers – *that* person will have a fruitful ministry. I have often spent days in prayer while waiting for the right words to reply to a letter as people have looked to me for help in their own ministry, or with personal difficulties. Think of the parable which bears on this in Luke 11:5-10.

'I tell you,' Jesus said, 'though he will not get up and give him the bread because he is his friend, yet because of the man's persistence, he will get up and give him as much as he needs.'

The Lord Jesus told his disciples they were his friends if they did what he commanded them (John 15:14). That applies to us, too. We are like that friend when we come to God, needing 'bread' to give to others. How much do we know of that kind of persistence in prayer for others?

17. Do we give proper emphasis to waiting on God in the way we teach others? How true that God is no respecter of persons! Like me, you have probably received great spiritual help and refreshment from someone young in the faith whose walk with Christ is vibrant. Sometimes this can contrast markedly with the lack of such spiritual help received when talking with a person of much greater maturity.

It is a contradiction to say we put our trust in God when we don't look to him for guidance and direction. Those who never learn to wait upon the Lord and have their thoughts shaped by him won't ever have that steady purpose and calm trust which leaders need. And without it they cannot exercise wise influence upon others in times of crisis and difficulty.

THE PRACTICE OF PRAYER

18. Personally, I find it a good thing to fast. I don't lay down rules for anyone in this matter, but I know it has been good for me to go without meals to get time for prayer. We often hear people say that they don't have enough time to pray, yet we think nothing of spending an hour or two in taking our meals. Why not try doing without sometime? I have found it such a benefit spiritually, and I believe our digestion benefits too!

19. If our vision of the unseen and eternal is to be kept bright and true, how important it is to be faithful in our daily personal communion with the Lord himself through praying and studying the Bible. It is only through this that we can be guarded from temptation and from the traps of the devil. And it is only this which will help us through times of depression or sorrow.

20. We should teach young believers how to pray and how to intercede, and we should work at developing this in them. In all else that we want to teach them, this can be overlooked, though it needs to have first place. But unless we ourselves are praying people, and truly alive to God in this holy warfare, we will never influence others to be. I am quite sure that the more we pray, the more we *want* to pray; I am also sure that the opposite is true.

THE MORE WE PRAY, THE MORE WE WANT TO PRAY

TRUE HUMILITY

21. 'To show true humility toward all' (Titus 3:2). Paul asks Titus to teach the need for patience, and tenderness of heart and of manner. 'A patient man has great understanding, but a quick-tempered man displays folly' (Proverbs 14:29). Lack of humility and of patience can really hinder a ministry and render fruitless a work which would otherwise bear all the marks of much effectiveness and ability.

22. God has told us that he is slow to anger. All Christians should work at developing a calm and patient spirit in the face of wrong and injustice; but this is a special need for those in spiritual leadership.

'Starting a quarrel is like breaching a dam, so drop the matter before a dispute breaks out' (Proverbs 17:14).

If at any time we find ourselves about to quarrel, it is so important that we seek grace to be kept from it, and instead give ourselves to quiet waiting on the Lord for his power and guidance. This is the only way we can be ready to deal with the faults and disputes of others without being caught up ourselves with an argumentative spirit.

23. When we see the way others behave, their weaknesses and faults, we can easily be impatient with them, and be contemptuous of them. We see the cruelty some of them inflict on others, and as we do not behave in that way ourselves, we can too quickly judge ourselves better than them. This was the mistake of the Pharisee in Luke 18: 9-14. He thanked God from his heart that he was better than others, but his attitude was wrong and the Lord condemned it. Our guilt is not gauged by our actions, but by whether we fall short of God's standards for us, bearing in mind the opportunity we have been given. A real grasp of this will help us form a true estimate of ourselves compared with others. It will give us a truer perspective of them, and make us honour them more as people for whom Christ died. This is a key to fruitful ministry.

> *WE CAN EASILY BE IMPATIENT AND CONTEMPTUOUS*

'HE HUMBLED HIMSELF'
24. The Son of God became Man. He had every right to people's obedience while he was on earth. He was the Creator, he was heir to the throne of David, and his personal character and conduct were completely beyond reproach. Each of these rights was not only ignored, but trampled underfoot, and the Lord never

asserted them by any appeal to power, divine or human.

He was put to death, and it looked to everyone as if his cause was lost. What an example to follow! May we have grace to respond like that. How different heavenly wisdom is from earthly wisdom. This is the way to true victory and fruitfulness; being self-assertive or demanding one's rights can only result in spiritual defeat and barrenness.

25. The only Christian life is the Christ-life worked out in relation to our own circumstances.

THE SECRET OF SUBMISSION

26. Have you ever had something taken away which you relied on, like your home or job, or a friendship, or your health? How important it is not to complain, or if it is brought about by the misdoings of other people, not to let our minds turn it over and over, for we can easily become bitter. Then instead of things working for good, they can work for our harm. Paul tells us in Romans 8:28 that 'in all things God works for the good of those who love him'. Note that it is not 'the good of those whom he loves', for he loves everyone. We need to love God practically, in our experience, and to keep a right attitude of quiet confidence in him and faithfulness to him. That is the secret of submission.

27. Are we able to take the lowly place if a misunderstanding arises? Can we cope with being slighted or hurt without wanting to justify ourselves? Can we humble ourselves under the mighty hand of God, relying on him to lift us up in due course (1 Peter 5:6)? That is faith in action.

SELF-DISCIPLINE

28. We need to have a sensitive conscience about how we use our time. The fact that many Christian workers aren't accountable to anyone for how they use their time can carry with it a temptation to laxity.

29. It's just as possible to be lazy when we have a fixed timetable or schedule. We can do the work in a slovenly manner without heart or preparation. We may be faithful when we are preparing to preach before a crowd, but I know for myself that I have needed to be watchful about a more careless attitude creeping in when I am preparing to teach half a dozen people. May we have grace to do our best every time and all the time.

30. When a group of young people first arrive on the mission field, it's very common for a few members of the group to become the more prominent ones through their ability, zeal or sheer personality. We find ourselves saying, 'That one is going to make a great success.' But it is wiser to wait and see. Often the most unnoticed and less-gifted ones

> *OFTEN THE LESS-GIFTED ONES BECOME THE SUCCESSES*

become the successes through sheer stickability, diligence and devotion.

31. I wonder if you've ever seen the picture of an ox or heifer standing between an altar and a plough with the words 'Ready for either' underneath? That is just what Ephraim was *not* (Hosea 10:11). He preferred an easy life to the idea of service that involved real sacrifice and toil. This was sad because Ephraim was originally intended for a special place of significance amongst the Tribes. But that special place, rightly understood, meant special burdens and even sufferings on behalf of others.

SUFFERING WHICH SHAPES US

32. If we sincerely love God, we must not be surprised if he allows us to be tried in some fierce and painful way, and by somebody whom we feel should know better. And the trial keeps on. It isn't just a storm that comes and then goes, but it keeps on and on.

I believe that the Lord is looking at us all the time; if we fight through by faith in Christ, although it is a sore conflict, then we shall be 'made partakers of the love of Christ' more fully. The writer to the Hebrews speaks of our 'sharing in Christ, if we hold firmly till the end the confidence we had at first' (Hebrews 3:14). That is a great principle. It starts with the time we first professed faith, and goes on to the end. Then the Lord says, 'Yes, this dear child of mine, through my grace, has won through; he has loved that young Christian, that man who caused him so much grief, whom I put alongside him. Now I can entrust him with much more.'

LOOKING BEYOND THE HERE AND NOW
33. Every Christian has particular duties to family, friends, work and local church, and it is right and proper that we devote the main part of our time and energy to these. However, it is vital that we keep and develop a prayerful and sympathetic interest in God's people and God's work everywhere.

Let's remember our Lord's invitation to his disciples to lift up their eyes, and look on the fields, and to pray to the Lord of the harvest for workers. Otherwise, the words of the old adage 'Out of sight, out of mind' will speedily become true.

NEEDING OTHERS, AND LEARNING FROM THEM
34. We must remember that we are part of the Body of Christ, and the Spirit of God works through that Body as a whole. No one, however senior, can say to another: 'I have no need of you.' We may not say this in so many words, yet the way we live can reflect that kind of attitude. It can suggest that we do not really consider ourselves inter-dependent, or needful of the prayerful judgement of other Christians.

35. We need to be so careful that we don't 'despise' the least of 'these little ones'. I recall being told as a teenager that young men needed to guard against thinking they knew it all. Now, years on, the temptation is different. Older people can think we have nothing to learn from younger people. And this is even worse. They have a wealth for us to appreciate, and to profit from.

36. The first recorded words of the Lord Jesus to his newly-made disciples were: 'Blessed are the poor in spirit, for theirs is the kingdom of heaven' (Matthew 5:3). And Paul writes, 'The man who thinks he knows something does not yet know as he ought to know' (1 Corinthians 8:2).

EXPERIENCE IN THE LORD'S WORK CAN BECOME A HINDRANCE

Experience in the Lord's work is a great blessing, but it can become a hindrance, if it is not accompanied with true humility or that holy 'poor spirit'. A younger and less-experienced person can help us see things in a new way. If we won't listen to him, then our own experience is preventing us from learning more; and God may want us to see something new in the situation.

Dixon Edward Hoste was a member of 'the Cambridge Seven', sailing to China in 1885. He married Gertrude Broomhall, niece of Hudson Taylor. Hoste took leadership of the China Inland Mission in 1900 amid the dark days of the Boxer Rebellion (1899-1901), and led the mission for 35 years.[4]

---

4. This dark period in China's history took the lives of thousands of Chinese Christians, as well as the lives of 58 CIM missionaries and 21 of the mission's children.

FIVE MARKS OF CHRISTIAN LEADERSHIP

John Stott

John Stott remains one of the best-known Christian leaders of recent times.[5] He described himself as a pastor, leader and friend. Our purpose here is to pull out from his work some of the advice he gave to younger leaders.

In everything, John Stott's twin authorities were the Person of Christ and scripture. He anchored himself in scripture as a 'daily dogged discipline'. For 25 years Stott led university missions around the world and never lost the heart of an evangelist. His global ministry had two main foci: students and pastors.

As is evident through his preaching and writing, he had wide intellectual reach, and curiosity about the world: the geographical world, the natural world, and the world of ideas.

On a human level, the sheer scale of his ministry was made possible by a unique partnership, unlikely to be repeated. Frances Whitehead (1925-2019) was at his side as his secretary for 55 years. In the words

---

5. Obituaries appeared in *The Times, The Telegraph, The Guardian* and *The Independent. The Oxford Dictionary of National Biography* carries an entry.

of Mark Labberton, Principal of Fuller Seminary, both were 'fast, exacting and determined'.[6] Both forsook marriage to give their lives to Stott's ministry. Their partnership will find 'a unique place in church history', said Chris Wright at the Thanksgiving service for Frances in All Souls.[7]

John Stott lived modestly in a two-roomed flat in London. The staffing for his ministry was equally modest: just himself and Frances, with the support of a succession of Study Assistants, who would use a desk in Stott's bedroom. This team of three formed the 'happy triumvirate'.[8]

In John Stott's writing or speaking on leadership, he cast his mind widely. Beyond church leaders and mission leaders there are parents, who lead families; school and university teachers and administrators; senior managers in business, in industry, in science and technology, law, medicine, and politics; and thought leaders in the professions and in the media. Student leaders, Stott observed, had, 'especially since the 1960s, exercised influence beyond their years and

---

6. See *John Stott's Right Hand: The untold story of Frances Whitehead*. Authorized biography by J E M Cameron. A story John Stott himself hoped would be told. (Expanded and updated edition, Dictum / Wipf and Stock, both 2020).

7. Chris Wright, International Ministries Director of Langham Partnership, preacher at the service in All Souls, Langham Place, London, 20 June 2019, to be found on Youtube.

8. A phrase borrowed from Charles Simeon (1759-1836), vicar of Holy Trinity Church, Cambridge for fifty years, whom Stott described as his mentor. See *Charles Simeon of Cambridge: Silhouettes and Skeletons*. Updated editions: Dictum, Wipf and Stock, both 2021. Ed J E M Cameron.

experience.' The biblical principles of leadership for all categories are the same.

Here are five areas he deemed essential for leaders:

1. VISION

We often talk of the role of a leader as 'to cast vision'. John Stott described vision as 'an act of seeing, an imaginative perception of things, combining insight and foresight.'[9] The instinct to cast vision will always go hand-in-hand with a sense of dissatisfaction. Being dissatisfied with the present, he said, is a *sine qua non* for leadership. The spiritual leader will, then, look past what is, to see what *could be*.

We need to understand our times, and study them under the lens of scripture. In learning to understand our times, John Stott coined the term 'double listening'. We must listen to the world, he said, as well as listening to the Word, while not giving them equal weight. By understanding the culture and trends of the times in this way, a leader can work to discern 'what to do' (see 1 Chronicles 12:32) – that is, what to aim for, and how to achieve it. Young rebels, he noted, can, over the decades, lapse into middle-class,

A VISIONARY LEADER WILL REMAIN TENACIOUS FOR TRUTH

---

9. *Issues Facing Christians Today*, (Marshall, Morgan and Scott, 1984) p328. Now available from Harper Collins, updated by Roy McCloughry.

middle-aged, middle-of-the-road mediocrity, but a visionary leader will remain tenacious for truth.

By the 1960s and 1970s, countries founded on the Judaeo-Christian ethic were starting to become deeply secular. This secularization showed starkly in, for example, abortion figures. The slide should, Stott said, give rise to outrage among Christian people, rather than to a resigned acceptance. Outrage of itself, he noted, provides no rallying cry. The visionary leader will point the way forward, and issue a call to follow in that way. We see in the biblical narrative how Moses led his people out of bondage in Egypt, and how Nehemiah gathered men to work with him in rebuilding the wall of Jerusalem.

John Stott immersed himself in the writing of the Apostle Paul. It was joked among students in All Souls who listened to him preach that he was clearer on the Apostle Paul than was the Apostle Paul! In the New Testament epistles we see the vision which characterized Paul's desire for the churches, his passion for the cause of the gospel, and his call for Christians to imitate his example as he follows Jesus Christ.

2. HARD WORK

Moses would have to gather the Israelites and form them into a nation, and lead them through perils and hardship in the desert before they would eventually reach the Promised Land. This would take single-mindedness, perseverance and endurance.

Nehemiah would have to gather materials and make plans for the rebuilding of the city wall, and head off his critics – again, needing single-mindedness, perseverance and endurance. The accounts of both these men's lives are detailed, for our learning.

The Apostle Paul wrote of how he 'laboured with all the energy Christ mightily worked' within him, and of his 'daily concern for all the churches'. An effective leader will work hard, and a pastor will never lose sight of the pastoral needs of those in his care.

Hudson Taylor, the missionary pioneer to China, spoke of any big work of God as having three stages: moving from seemingly 'Impossible' through the long stage of 'Difficult', and finally to 'Done'. To get from 'Impossible to 'Done' will require much slog, and continued reliance on God.

As well as citing spiritual leaders, John Stott would take examples of remarkable leaders from history. Two stories he would tell are those of the British Prime Minister, Winston Churchill, and the Oxford motor manufacturer, Lord Nuffield.

Winston Churchill, Prime Minister during World War II, was under no illusion as to what victory over the Nazis would cost. Churchill announced in his first speech to Parliament on 13 May 1940, that he had 'nothing to offer but blood, toil, tears and sweat' and that it would take 'many months of struggle and suffering'.[10]

---

10. The classic biography of Churchill is by Martin Gilbert (Minerva, 1992)

Lord Nuffield, born Will Morris, who left school aged 14 to be apprenticed to an Oxford bicycle repairer, became the greatest UK philanthropist of the 20th century.[11] His money was made through Morris cars, and the initials MG (Morris Garage) are still known today. He did not like it when people referred to his being 'lucky'. While he was clearly shrewd in his business dealings, and had natural gifts and abilities, his fortune was made, he said, through sheer hard work.

3. THE ABILITY TO PRESS ON

Moses withstood ongoing criticism from his people in the wilderness. They challenged his authority, built the golden calf, complained about the water and the manna, and could have risen in mutiny. A lesser man would have given up, but Moses could not do that. He pressed on in the face of discouragement. These were God's covenant people whom he would lead by God's promise into the land flowing with milk and honey.

The Apostle Paul offers the supreme example of a leader who never lost sight

THE APOSTLE PAUL NEVER LOST SIGHT OF HIS GOAL

of his goal or purpose. Even when close to death, and feeling deserted by friends, (2 Timothy 1:15; 4:16) he was as clear-sighted and heavenly-sighted as ever. 'I have fought the good fight, I have finished the race, I

---

11. Founder of Nuffield College, Oxford and a major donor to the university and the city. Nuffield Trust / Nuffield Foundation provide significant resources for scientific and medical research.

have kept the faith... and now there is in store for me the crown of righteousness – not only for me but for all those who long for his appearing.' (2 Timothy 4:7,8).

In speaking of the ability to press on, John Stott would tell the stories of William Wilberforce and Charles Simeon, friends and contemporaries. Wilberforce was single-minded and unwavering in his desire to see the abolition of the slave trade. He looked implausible, small and unprepossessing. His struggle for abolition took him forty-five years, and included such ill-health that he had to retire from Parliament and continue to fight from outside. The UK government would pay £20m in compensation to slave traders. It was a remarkable victory. Simeon was vicar of Holy Trinity Church, Cambridge and at first was so hated by his congregation that they locked him out of his church. But he pressed on and persevered, and when he died there were long queues of 'gownsmen' (students and faculty) to get into his funeral; shops were closed; and the streets were lined in his honour.[12]

4. SELF-DISCIPLINE

Leadership can be a lonely place, and the Bible gives insights into the ways the great leaders laid hold of God's promises to sustain them. The first discipline of spiritual leaders is to guard their spiritual life.

---

12. Charles Simeon had remarkable influence on the Church of England. Its ripples are still evident. John Stott took the wording of Simeon's memorial plaque in Holy Trinity Church for his own headstone. He said that it was Simeon, through his writings, who taught him how to preach.

Stott would draw attention to the Lord speaking with Moses as a man speaks to a friend; and how the Psalms show the way David found in God not only his shepherd, but his light and salvation, his rock and the stronghold of his life. John Stott would take leaders to the gospels showing Christ himself spending time in prayer, away from the crowds, and again in Gethsemane, as the disciples slept.

Stott rose early each day, and after listening to the news, he would read and pray. For more than fifty years he used the McCheyne Bible Reading Plan, which takes people through the whole Bible in a year, and the New Testament and Psalms twice.[13] 'Nothing, he wrote, 'has helped me more than this to grasp the grand themes of the Bible.'

Keeping spiritually fresh is vital, and spiritual disciplines will only ever mean 'daily, dogged discipline'. Human frailty, human forgetfulness, even disregard of people and places and situations which need our prayer, will always pull very strongly. The devil will do all he can to deflect people from praying.

For John Stott, self-discipline did not mean working all the time; far from it. As God gave rhythms of work and rest, so a Christian should reflect that pattern. Stott enjoyed bird-watching, and he coined the term 'orni-theology' to

> **SELF-DISCIPLINE DID NOT MEAN WORKING ALL THE TIME**

---

13. See his introduction to the reading plan, included in *Authority and Joy: the Bible in your life*, John Stott and Sinclair Ferguson (Dictum 2021).

describe his study of them. He personally photographed some 2,500 species of birds, and used his own photographs to illustrate his book *The Birds our Teachers*.[14] His refreshment and recreation included family time, getting to know his nieces, and in due course their children. He would go frequently to The Hookses, his writing retreat in Pembrokeshire, and he and Frances would transfer the office there for several weeks in the summer. They would be joined by friends, and after the day's work, evenings would be spent relaxing together.

John Stott planned his time carefully, for pastoral work, for preparation, for writing, for travelling. In his years as Rector of All Souls, he would regularly take a day away from the office to think and pray, and to engage with major issues or questions. This could be as often as once a week in demanding times. It proved invaluable.

5. AN ATTITUDE OF SERVICE

For a Christian in leadership, the principle of serving applies, whether in the Christian or secular arenas. Part II of this book elaborates on Christian leadership in a secular context.

The Lord himself showed the contrast between a Christian spirit of serving, and the way leaders of the day 'lorded it' over the Gentiles. The Son of Man came to serve, rather than to be served, and to give his life on the cross.

---

14. Published by Hendrickson Publishers, 1999.

Scripture warns that leaders must not become proud. The Pharisees loved titles. Christian leaders who are concerned for their position and their job titles are in spiritual danger (see Matthew 23:1-12). On Christ's last evening on earth before he was crucified, he clothed himself in humility, as he washed his disciples' feet (John 13). What a picture to leave with them, and with the Church down the ages. It should never be below the dignity of leaders to serve those whom they lead; it is a leader's duty.

LEADERS MUST NOT BECOME PROUD

So Christian leaders will see the authority delegated to them as a means to serve. While it is right for them to be respected, and obeyed when their authority demands that, they themselves will always be looking to the interests of others. We come back to our supreme example, Christ himself. 'Your attitude should be the same as that of Jesus Christ' wrote the Apostle Paul: 'who ... made himself nothing, taking the very nature of a servant – and became obedient to death, even death on a cross!' (Philippians 2:1-11).

One mark of Christians who desire to serve is their willingness to learn from others. This will show itself in specific situations, but it is more widely discernible in how people live, and in what they read. John read widely, learning from secular writers and from Christians around the world, past and present. His book *People my Teachers* introduces a selection of those from whom he learned. They include the

Apostle Paul, Richard Wurmbrand, Mohandas Ghandi, Hudson Taylor, Ernest Shackleton and Charles Darwin.

Finally, John Stott advocated that where possible, leadership should be in the hands of a team rather than an individual, while clearly there must be a 'first among equals', who bears the final authority. Members of a team complement one another, and encourage one another. Team leadership, Stott pointed out, protects the leader from veering into 'excessive individualism, extreme isolation, and self-centred empire building'. Further, members of a team are accountable to one another. There are sad stories of leaders who have been overcome by temptation in financial matters, or in errant sexual behaviour. They have often worked largely on their own and have not been held accountable by co-workers, or been overseen in a meaningful way by a mission agency (or, in a church context, by the eldership or church council). Mutual accountability, such as a leadership team provides, will help guard against this.

John Stott submitted to an Accountability Group of Elders as he made decisions on how to spend his time. To have a group like this, who are spiritually-minded, who understand the ministry, and who can bring an objectivity to their counsel is liberating, rather than constricting. The way of a fool seems right to him, but a wise man listens to advice. (Proverbs 12:15).

John Stott (1921-2011) was Rector, then Rector Emeritus, of All Souls, Langham Place, London. He founded EFAC, LICC and Langham Partnership International.[15] *'Uncle John' as he was known around the world, wrote over 50 books. For more, see his entry in the* Oxford Dictionary of National Biography.[16]

[Compiled by the Editor]

---

15. Evangelical Fellowship in the Anglican Communion (EFAC); London Institute for Contemporary Christianity (LICC); Langham Partnership, which brings together three ministries: training in preaching; distribution of literature; and the provision of scholarships.

16. And in this series: *John Stott: Pastor, Leader, Friend* by Chris Wright, Lindsay Brown et al. John Stott was Chief Architect of the landmark *Lausanne Covenant* (1974). This document would define evangelicalism for the remainder of the century.

THE LEADER AS SERVANT

Ajith Fernando

Foreword to the 2006 Edition
(An Authentic Servant)

The Apostle Paul's farewell to the Ephesian elders at Miletus (Acts 20:17-38) is deeply moving. Many leaders find themselves turning to this passage again and again. In v28 we read of how Paul urges the elders to keep watch over themselves, as well as the flock. Perhaps one of the truest indicators of our spiritual leadership is how we do that, and what we pray for ourselves.

Spiritual leadership is a serious responsibility, and some carry that responsibility from their student years. Both of us had the privilege of leading a student Christian Union, and we trust this booklet will be used and talked about by student leaders now, as well as by church leaders, mission leaders, home group leaders, youth pastors, mission leaders…

In these pages, Ajith Fernando cuts to the heart of the matter, raising critical questions often lost in our cultures of comfort. Are we willing for costly service? Do we yearn for those whom we lead? How can we keep our focus on the crops, and let the paradox of joy in suffering seep down into our understanding, our personal discipleship? There is no other authentic Christian leadership. Because of our fallen natures, and the pride with permeates all our attitudes and relationships, we are bound to struggle – and to find ourselves continually struggling – if we are to win through to true servanthood.

We commend this booklet to you, and trust it will come as a great encouragement as you seek to live in Christ's service.

Patrick Fung, *General Director, OMF International*

Lindsay Brown, *[Then] General Secretary, IFES*

THE LEADER AS SERVANT

Ajith Fernando

The Apostle Paul led as one who serves. He wrote to the Christians in Corinth, 'Death is at work in us, but life is at work in you.' In spiritual ministry, we are called to die for the sake of others. Are we willing for that?

Even a superficial look at the New Testament would show us that the cross of suffering is an essential part of Christian ministry. We can safely say that if we try to get round that, we will forfeit eternal fruitfulness. I think this is an emphasis that has been neglected in contemporary thinking about Christian service. We live in a society that places much emphasis on comfort, convenience, entertainment and good feelings. And because the emphasis on suffering is so much at odds with this emphasis, we seem to have avoided it.

BEING WILLING TO DIE

Jesus said, 'Love each other as I have loved you' (John 15:12). Jesus explained how we do this, saying, 'Greater love has no one than this, that he lay down his life for his friends' (John 15:13). Christians are people who are so committed to their 'friends' - those they minister among - that they lay down their lives for them. This is the fundamental difference between the kind of commitment Jesus calls us to, and the world's commitment. Jesus' exposition of the Good Shepherd in John 10 shows that. Jesus says that, when the wolf comes, the hired hand abandons the sheep and runs away (10:12,13). But the Good Shepherd is not like that. He lays down his life for the sheep.

And we are to follow his example! When Christ died on the cross, he paid the penalty for the sins of the whole world. Such a price we finite and sinful individuals cannot pay. We are called to love 'one another' a group less than everyone in the world. John 15:13 says Jesus died for his friends. In the same way we, too, are to die for our friends. That is a smaller group of people for whom we have special responsibility like our family, our congregation, and the people we work with.

First among the friends we die for are our family members. Paul says, 'Husbands, love your wives just as Christ loved the Church, and gave himself up for her' (Ephesians 5:25). Most wives would say, 'I don't want my husband to die for me. Just tell him to talk to me!' Talking when you are very tired is a kind of death. When we come back after a heavy day's ministry, and we are exhausted, we prefer not to talk. If there has been tension in the home, and we know that if we bring the subject up it will lead to a conversation of an hour or two, we prefer to avoid that. Part of our Christian commitment is to die to that desire not to talk.

So laying down our lives can mean many things. Most of us are not called literally to die for our friends. This example from family life shows that our calling may be subtler. We may be called to endure frustration, discomfort, tiredness and pain because of others. That is not easy for us in this pragmatic age, especially because our society is so skilled at finding ways to avoid this kind of inconvenience.

> *LAYING DOWN OUR LIVES CAN MEAN MANY THINGS*

Even Christians can be swayed by the prevailing mood that gives such a high place to convenience and ease. We, too, can make our choices in ways that avoid frustration, discomfort and pain. For example, when deciding where to serve, among our primary considerations could be the benefits offered like the salary, accommodation and pension. We hear people saying, 'I don't want to work in that country, because I don't like the climate.' When someone we work with becomes difficult, we could just drop that person. When those we are called to reach, for example the Muslims in a given area, persistently reject the gospel, we could just leave the area and go to a more receptive area. All this is alien to the basic call of Christ to discipleship. That was a call to deny ourselves, take up a cross and follow him (Mark 8:34). And a cross is a place where people die.

A THEOLOGY OF GROANING

My basic premise is that when we are committed to the people we are called to serve, we will inevitably suffer pain by sticking to this commitment. Let's see how Paul illustrated this principle. The first thing we must note is that Paul regarded groaning as an essential feature of life in a fallen world. This is a world subjected to frustration because of the Fall (Romans 8:20).

Because of this, even those who belong to God join the rest of creation in groaning. Of course for us this groaning is 'as in the pains of childbirth'— the anticipatory groan of those who look forward to a coming glory (Romans 8:22-23). He says, 'Our present sufferings are not worth comparing with the glory that will be revealed in us' (Romans 8:18). Once after listing a huge catalogue of trials, Paul says, 'We do not lose heart ... for our light and momentary troubles are achieving for us an eternal glory that far outweighs them all' (2 Corinthians 4:16-17). So we have a theology of groaning.

The heavenly vision, however, enables us to groan with positive anticipation, and helps us to stay on in difficult situations. I don't

> *THERE IS NO EASY SITUATION FOR A DISCIPLE OF CHRIST*

want to criticize people who leave difficult situations. God has called each of us to serve in different places, and there is no such thing as an easy situation for a disciple of Christ. But I think it is sad to see such a large number of Christians leaving situations of obvious conflict and hardship. Christians are people who can stay on in such situations because they are not afraid to groan. This is part of our theology. Because we groan with the joyous anticipation of glory, we are willing to live with frustration when our calling includes that.

YEARNING FOR THE LOST

Once you have accepted groaning as an essential part of life, then you have the strength to yearn for people. We yearn firstly for the lost. Paul expresses this yearning in Romans 9:1-3, 'I have great sorrow and unceasing anguish in my heart. For I could wish that I myself were cursed and cut off from Christ, for the sake of my own race….' You can see how the yearning has produced hurt in him. As he contemplated the lostness of his own people he was broken up inside. Today people do all they can to avoid such pain. I believe this is one reason why so many Christians ignore or reject the doctrine of lostness of people outside Christ. They don't want to face the pain that such a doctrine will bring. Charles Spurgeon discusses those who say, 'I could not rest comfortably if I believed the orthodox doctrine about the ruin of men.' Spurgeon's response to this is: 'Most true. But what right have we to rest comfortably?'

So because yearning produces pain, people avoid yearning too. In fact this yearning is a missing factor in ministry today. But it is yearning that produces urgency in ministry. This is expressed in 1 Corinthians 9:16: 'I am compelled to preach. Woe to me if I do not preach the gospel!'

IT IS YEARNING THAT PRODUCES URGENCY

He was passionate for the gospel. The rest of this chapter expresses how this passion caused Paul to forfeit the rights of an apostle and make so many adjustments to his lifestyle in order that he may reach as many people as possible. Imagine hearing this highly-educated Pharisee who was also a Roman citizen say, 'Though I am free and belong to no man, I make myself a slave to everyone to win as many as possible' (1 Corinthians 9:19). He climaxes this description with the unforgettable words, 'I have become all things to all men so that by all possible means I might save some' (9:22).

Today we are afraid of such urgency. Perhaps people we have trusted and yearned for have hurt us. Perhaps projects that we earnestly gave ourselves to ended in failure resulting in disappointment and humiliation. So we don't want to break through that protective shield that we have built around our emotions, because it makes us too vulnerable to pain. That's why we don't yearn for people with the urgency that Paul had.

There was a time when urgency was one of the things that attracted people to the gospel. It is said that Benjamin Franklin would go to hear George Whitefield preach because there before his eyes he could watch a person burn with passion. Today instead of urgency we have excellent programming, entertainment, and the promise of temporal blessings to attract people. In a generation dedicated to feeling good, we will avoid pain at all costs.

YEARNING FOR BELIEVERS

Just as we yearn for the lost until they come to Christ, we yearn for believers until Christ is formed in them. Using the vivid imagery of a woman in labour, Paul expresses this in Galatians 4:19: 'My dear children, for whom I am again in the pains of childbirth until Christ is formed in you, how I wish I could be with you and change my tone, because I am perplexed about you!' He identified so much with the Galatians that he *hurt* over their theological confusion.

We hear a lot of talk about incarnational ministry today. But incarnation and pain are inseparable. When we cross the barrier from professionalism into yearning, we find that yearning brings hurting with it. I am surprised at how often people express relief over the breaking of some commitment they have. Maybe it is a difficult spouse or a difficult church, or difficult people. They move away from that spouse or church or those people, and save themselves from so much stress and pain. It is almost as if liberation from pain or stress is regarded as a sign of God's will in this decision. The biblical Christian accepts such pain as an essential part of commitment to people.

In 1 Thessalonians 2:8 Paul describes what lies behind this type of commitment. 'We loved you so much that we were delighted to share with you not only the gospel of God but our lives as well.' The verb translated 'loved you' is a very rare word. It doesn't occur often in the New Testament or in other Greek literature. It means 'we longed for you, or yearned for you'. Some translations have 'being affectionately desirous of you'. Paul goes on to talk of sharing 'not only the gospel of God, but our lives as well'. The word translated 'lives' is *psyche*, which means 'soul', or 'inner being'. Paul yearned for people so much that he opened his inner being to them. He had crossed from professionalism into yearning.

The result of such opening of our lives in this way is that we develop leaders. Paul describes how he opened his life to Timothy in 2 Timothy 3:10: 'You... know all about my teaching, my way of life, my purpose, faith, patience, love, endurance, persecutions, sufferings.' Through this opening up of Paul's life, Timothy knew all about Paul. So when he went to Corinth, Paul was able to say of him, 'He will remind you of my way of life in Christ Jesus...' (1 Corinthians 4:17). Paul was telling them that if they want to know what he thinks and does, they should find out from Timothy. Through opening himself in this way, Paul had reproduced himself and developed Timothy and a host of other leaders.

BIBLICAL STRESS
One of the results of opening our lives to others and yearning for them is stress. Paul described this in 2 Corinthians 11:28, 29: 'Besides everything else, I face

daily the pressure of my concern for all the churches. Who is weak, and I do not feel weak? Who is led into sin, and I do not inwardly burn?' Today there is a lot of talk and many books about stress, and how to avoid it. I have found some of the books very helpful because often I take on stress for the wrong reasons.

A lot of stress today is caused by us not taking our Sabbath rest in this fast-paced society. Rest is an important aspect of the biblical lifestyle. Sometimes stress comes as a result of intense competitiveness. Driven people who find their primary fulfilment in success in this competitive society experience unbiblical stress because there is no guarantee of constant earthly success in this fallen world. Perhaps we suffer more than we dare admit from a 'Messiah complex' resulting in us refusing to delegate responsibilities to others. Thus we end up doing things that others could have done and bearing burdens which we should have shared with others. This also means we lose out on nurturing others, who would learn much from sharing our workload.

> **PEOPLE WHO FIND THEIR FULFILMENT IN SUCCESS EXPERIENCE UNBIBLICAL STRESS**

A lot of our stress, then, is not biblical. Biblical stress comes out of a love for others, not a lust for achievement. It is the inevitable result of identifying so closely with people that we begin to bear their burdens.

STRENGTH FOR TAKING ON STRESS

If we are to take on biblical stress, we must first be strong enough to endure it. The strength for this comes from the joy of the Lord. There is an interesting sequence in John 15 that brings this out. In verses 12 and 13, Jesus gives his famous challenge to sacrificial love: 'Love each other as I have loved you. Greater love has no one than this: that he lay down his life for his friends.' But just before that he said, 'I have told you this so that my joy may be in you, and your joy may be complete' (John 15:11). Having the joy of the Lord in our lives is crucial. In fact I would say it is a fundamental requirement for effective ministry.

The Epistle to the Philippians shows that Paul's joy was incomplete when there was no unity in the church (Philippians 2:2; 4:2). What we have said so far makes it clear that we will lose a lot of joy over things on earth because of the love we have for others. But there is one type of joy – the joy of the Lord - that we must ensure that we always have. So Paul says in Philippians 4:4, 'Rejoice in the Lord always. I will say it again: Rejoice!' The repetition indicates the importance of jealously guarding this joy.

> *JOY IS A REQUIREMENT FOR EFFECTIVE MINISTRY*

Paul goes on to describe how we guard the joy of the Lord. He first says, 'Let your gentleness be evident to all' (4:5). When the joy of the Lord is missing, gentleness goes, and we can become bitter about the way we have been treated in difficult situations.

Then if provoked, we can react in an ungentle way. How, then, do we get this joy which will make us gentle? The answer is simple. 'Do not be anxious about anything' (4:6). We may have the stress of love, but we can't have the anxiety of unbelief. Now that is easy to say, but not so easy to achieve. Paul goes on to describe how we can do it when he says, '...but in everything, by prayer and petition, with thanksgiving, present your requests to God' (Philippians 4:6). The 'but' here is a strong word (*alla* in the Greek). He is presenting an alternative course of action. In other words, we grapple with God in prayer until we have cast our burden on him. Then the burden is handed over to God. We are released from its power over us, and from our fear. Our joy is restored.

The result is that 'the peace of God, which transcends all understanding, will guard your hearts and your minds in Christ Jesus' (Philippians 4:7). This peace, like the joy of the Lord, is essential to life. Paul says it guards our hearts and minds. So we grapple with God until joy and peace in believing returns. Only then can we go to a torn world and take on the stress we need to absorb, in order to be agents of God's healing.

> *WE GRAPPLE WITH GOD UNTIL OUR JOY IS RESTORED*

PRESERVING JOY

George Mueller retired from running his orphanages at the age of 70, and then spent 17 more years as an itinerant evangelist. He was once asked the causes for such a long and happy life. One of the causes he gave was the joy he felt in God and in his work. Elsewhere he wrote that the first great and primary business to which he ought to attend every day was to have his soul happy in the Lord.

Grappling to preserve the joy of the Lord is a discipline we ought to cultivate. There is an example of this from the life of Hudson Taylor just after his first wife, Maria, had died. He first went upstairs to his room and spent time alone with God, then he came down to see to the funeral arrangements. When it was time to close the coffin, he took one last look at his beloved wife, and went up to his room to be alone with God. Only after this did he come back to complete the burial procedures.

John Stam of the China Inland Mission was shot along with his wife, Betty, by the Communists, when they were 29 and 30 years old. John once said, 'Take away everything I have, but do not take away the sweetness of walking and talking with the King of Glory'. The joy of the Lord was the one thing he could not be without.

God taught me this principle when I was having a hard time with my studies at university. I was doing a degree in biology, and it was a bad choice of subject as I am very weak with my hands. When dissecting, I would cut what I was supposed to leave, and leave behind what I was supposed to cut! And I can't draw at all. One third of our grade went for the practical lab work, and that was a disaster area for me. Besides, my heart was in the ministry, and I was longing to give my time for that. I often encountered depression and deep discouragement during those days. Later on I realized it had been a great privilege to be in that place. It was a Buddhist university with a vice-chancellor who was a Buddhist monk, and I was living in a Buddhist home. This, and the frustration of studying biology, was all part of my training for ministry. But it was difficult to go through at the time.

During this time I developed the discipline of walking, sometimes two or three miles, until I felt the joy of the Lord return. I had to come to grips with the situation, and let the belief in God's sovereignty break through into my life again. Only when this happened would I return home. On the walk back, I would intercede for others. But there was no intercession until the grappling with God was complete.

> *I DEVELOPED THE DISCIPLINE OF WALKING*

One of the greatest tragedies I see in ministry today is the number of angry Christian leaders there are who have lost their spiritual freshness. Sooner or later the weight of their anger shows in an ineffective and unattractive ministry. We must work at having our lives controlled by joy, not by anger. Angry people cannot be gentle under provocation. Any kind of provocation acts as a switch to release hidden anger. When we have joy in the Lord, however, the joy becomes our strength (Nehemiah 8:10). No earthly problem can take away that kind of joy. It becomes the most important thing in life, and we are able to remain strong because of it, in the midst of a crisis.

Sri Lanka is a country torn by strife between the Sinhala majority and the Tamil minority. We've also had a revolution by a group of Sinhala young people who tried to overthrow the government. There will be times when we have strong anger at what is happening, but that anger has to co-exist with the joy of the Lord. This came to a head for me in 1989. That year alone, we lost more than 50,000 people as a result of the Sinhala youth rebellion. There was never a time when there wasn't a dead body floating down the river at the edge of our city. And they were all young people. I knew some of those who died, and I was very angry.

The government set up a commission to inquire about why the young people are revolting. They asked interested people to make submissions to the commission. I felt this was a good time to express my outrage. We brought our staff together and prepared what turned out to be a very revolutionary document. We sent it to the commission. Some people who spoke out against the government at that time had been killed, including a leading journalist. After sending that document, I got up in the night a few times in a cold sweat, thinking they had come to take me. I felt it was my Christian responsibility to express this anger in a constructive way. But I soon realized that I was not handling my anger properly.

> *I GOT UP IN A COLD SWEAT, THINKING THEY HAD COME TO TAKE ME*

Many were leaving the country at this time, especially because of their children, as the schools were closed for long periods. My wife and I decided that whatever happened, we were not going to leave Sri Lanka. But wouldn't our children have a deprived upbringing? We concluded that if we kept a happy and contented home for our children, they would not be deprived in the ultimate sense. But my bad moods were not helping with this resolve. One day my wife said to the children so that I could hear, 'Father is in a bad mood. Let's hope he goes and reads his Bible.'

She had hit upon a very important theological truth. She knew that at this time when we were surrounded by anger, pain and death and the smell of bodies burning, we needed to spend time in the Word. Placed, as we were, in terrible temporal situations, we needed to expose ourselves to eternal truth and to focus on things that do not change. Then we would get strength, and with that strength joy would come: the joy that enables us to go out to the world and to take on the pain of other people. Another reason that George Mueller gave for his long and happy life was the love he felt for the Scriptures and the constant recuperative power they exercised upon his whole being.

MOVING FROM GOD TO PEOPLE

Christian ministers are people who get their strength from God. With his joy in our hearts, we will be able to take blows that come our way from angry people. If you hit the stomach of a strong person, he hardly feels it. If you hit a weak person, it can come like a hammer blow. We must become strong in this way by strengthening our spiritual muscles with the Lord's joy. This is essential if we are to be agents of reconciliation in this world.

During a time of conflict in our ministry, the Lord taught me a very important principle: before you meet with people, first meet with God. Our ministry springs primarily from God's acceptance of us.

> BEFORE YOU MEET WITH PEOPLE, FIRST MEET WITH GOD

I tell our staff in Youth for Christ that Christian ministers are those who first get their strength by being with God, and then go into the world to get bashed around. Then they come back, get strength from God, and go back into the world to get bashed around again. That is our life. We get strength, then we go and get bashed, get strength, go get bashed, get strength....

MOTIVATION TO MINISTRY

A lot of motivation to and marketing of ministry and missions today focuses on the excitement involved in the work. But that could result in people coming to serve who do not expect the inevitable suffering that will come with it. This is why I believe that the more important features for our marketing of Christian ministry should be those unchanging truths that drive us to be involved in ministry. Foremost among these is the content of the gospel that tells of eternal salvation to those who accept it and eternal damnation to those who reject it. Such truths remain the same when there are problems and when things are going fine. When Christians come fired with a passion for people based on such awesome, unchanging truths, then they will not give up or get disillusioned when the going gets tough.

The different statements of the Great Commission, which was Jesus' way of motivating his disciples to missions, include in them different aspects of the content of the gospel. For example, Luke 24:46-47 says 'This is what is written: The Christ will suffer and rise from the dead on the third day, and repentance and forgiveness will be preached in his name to all nations.' The content of the gospel itself was part of the Great Commission.

The great Scottish theologian James Denney once spoke at a missions conference, and almost his whole talk was on propitiation. Those who invited him were wondering what on earth he was up to, talking on propitiation at a missions conference. And just in his conclusion, he said that if propitiation is a reality *then* we must go and preach the gospel to the whole world. Let people see the horror of life without God and the glory of what the gospel can do to change that. Then they will be willing to pay the price that is required in order to take the gospel to people everywhere. So we focus on the great gospel and call people to be willing to die for it.

THE GLORY OF THE GOSPEL

In a world where physical health, appearance, and convenience have gained almost idolatrous prominence, God may be calling Christians to demonstrate the glory of the gospel by being joyful and content while enduring pain and hardship. People who are unfulfilled after pursuing things that do not satisfy may be astonished to see Christians who are joyful and content after depriving themselves for the gospel. This may be a new way to demonstrate the glory of the gospel to this hedonistic culture.

I have a great fear for the church. The West is fast becoming an unreached region. The Bible and history show that suffering is an essential ingredient in reaching unreached people. Will the loss of a theology of suffering lead the Western church to become ineffective in evangelism? The church in the East is growing, and because of that God's servants are suffering. Significant funding and education come to the East from the West. With funding and education comes influence. Could Westerners influence Eastern Christians to abandon the Cross by communicating that they must be doing something wrong if they suffer in this way? Christians in both the East and the West need to have a firm theology of suffering if they are to be healthy and bear fruit.

> CHRISTIANS NEED TO HAVE A FIRM THEOLOGY OF SUFFERING

Christians from affluent countries may be losing their ability to live with inconvenience, stress and hardship, as there is more and more emphasis on comfort and convenience. Many are unable to stick to their commitments when the going gets tough. They leave their places of service, change churches, and discard their friends. Some discard their spouses far too soon when their marriages face problems. What will this mean for the church in the West? Might the West soon disqualify itself from being a missionary-sending region? I think we are seeing some embarrassing examples.

Students often ask me, 'How can I prepare to be a missionary?' I usually answer by urging them to stick to the group they are part of, and to go through the pain of being there without giving up. That will make them skilled in facing the frustration and pain that is an unavoidable aspect of the missionary call. There is an unprecedented amount of study today on cultural anthropology and contextualization, and I praise God for that. These studies are very helpful for incarnational ministry. But more helpful even than that is the ability to die, to die for those we are called to work with: our families, our churches and our mission fields.

DRIVENNESS OR SERVANTHOOD?

I have a large group of people to whom I write asking for prayer when I have a need. Sometimes my need is overcoming tiredness. When I write about this, many write back saying they are praying that God would strengthen me and guide me in my scheduling. However, there are differences in the way friends from the East and some from the West respond. I get the strong feeling that many in the West think struggling with tiredness from overwork is evidence of disobedience to God. My contention is that

> **THERE ARE DIFFERENCES IN THE WAY FRIENDS FROM THE EAST AND WEST RESPOND**

it is wrong if one gets sick from overwork through drivenness and insecurity. But we may have to endure tiredness when we, like Paul, are servants of people.

The New Testament is clear that those who work for Christ will suffer because of their work. Tiredness, stress, and strain may be the cross God calls us to. Paul often spoke about the physical hardships his ministry brought him, including emotional strain (Galatians 4:19; 2 Corinthians 11:28); anger (2 Corinthians 11:29); sleepless nights and hunger (2 Corinthians 6:5); affliction and perplexity (2 Corinthians 4:8); and toiling – working to the point of weariness (Colossians 1:29). In statements radically countercultural in today's 'body conscious' society, he said, 'Though our outer self is wasting away, our inner self is being renewed day by day' (2 Corinthians 4:16); and, 'For we who live are always being given over to death for Jesus' sake, so that the life of Jesus also may be manifested in our mortal flesh. So death is at work in us, but life in you' (2 Corinthians 4:11-12). I fear that many Christians approach these texts only with an academic interest, not seriously asking how the verses should apply in their lives.

The West, having struggled with the tyrannical rule of time, has a lot to teach the East about the need for rest. The East has something to teach the West about embracing physical problems that come from commitment to people. If you think it is wrong to suffer physically because of ministry, then you suffer more from the problem than those who believe that suffering is an inevitable step on the path to fruitfulness and fulfilment. Since the Cross is a basic aspect of discipleship, the church must train Christian leaders to expect pain and hardship. When this perspective enters our minds, pain will not touch our joy and contentment in Christ. In 18 different New Testament passages, suffering and joy appear together. In fact, suffering is often the cause for joy (Romans 5:3-5; Colossians 1:24; James 1:2-3).

SUFFERING IS OFTEN THE CAUSE FOR JOY

A DOORWAY TO DISILLUSIONMENT?

Sometimes when I present a challenge similar to what I have given here, sincere Christians fear that I may be encouraging people to live an unbalanced Christian life. They point to many who 'killed themselves' for the gospel but who in the process neglected their health and their families. They are now very disillusioned as they struggle with physical and spiritual burnout, bitter spouses, rebellious children and a sense of defeat at the end of their ministries. Indeed it is important for us to look after our health, as Christianity is concerned with the physical aspects of life too. But I think the Bible does leave room for situations where we will suffer physically owing to our commitment. Paul said, 'Though outwardly we are wasting away, yet inwardly we are being renewed day by day' (2 Corinthians 4:16). People who are being renewed inwardly would not end up disillusioned. Certainly disillusionment would not be God's will for his faithful servants.

STAYING STRONG
I believe that we would end our ministries well, and without disillusionment if, in addition to taking up the cross, we follow other basic features of biblical discipleship:
- regular unhurried time with God in prayer and Bible study
- guarding the joy of the Lord
- taking our Sabbath rest
- working with the body by delegating responsibilities to others without trying to meet every need
- sacrificially fulfilling our responsibilities to our families
- looking forward to the coming glory which enables us to live with frustration on earth

If you neglect these features, don't even try to die for the cause of the gospel. You will suffer some sad consequences because of the neglect. If you take up these features, and others that obedience to Christ involves, you will be stretched to the fullest and often brought to the end of yourself, but God will see you through, and life will become a thrilling adventure. You will demonstrate through your life that 'the one who calls you is faithful and he will do it' (1 Thessalonians 5:24). Just after making his call to take up the cross, Jesus said, 'For whoever wants to save his life will lose it, but whoever loses his life for me and the gospel will save it' (Mark 8:35).

God bless you as you seek to bring glory to the Lord Jesus Christ. You may be leading a large church, or a small Bible study group; you may be an elder or a youth worker; you may be an evangelist invited to speak on platforms, or you may be working to bring the light of Christ into a tough professional environment; you may be leading a mission agency, or leading a student fellowship on campus. In whatever place of influence God has set you, you have a serious calling and a high calling. May you finish well.

> *YOU HAVE A SERIOUS CALLING AND A HIGH CALLING*

Ajith Fernando, author and widely-used Bible expositor, joined the staff of Youth for Christ in Sri Lanka in 1976, serving first as National Director then Teaching Director. He and his wife, Nelun, are members of a church in Colombo consisting mainly of poor, urban first-generation Christians.

LEADERS WHO LAST

Vaughan Roberts

Vaughan Roberts goes to the kernel of spiritual leadership. Here, in a sense, is its irreducible minimum: 'spiritual leadership in your pocket'.

I had two surprises when I started out as a pastor. *First*, it was even better than I had imagined. I was actually being paid to do what I longed to do above anything else: tell people about Jesus and teach the Bible! *Secondly*, it was much harder than I'd anticipated. The sense of the privilege and importance of my work was exhilarating, but it was also exhausting.

> IT WAS EXHILARATING, BUT IT WAS ALSO EXHAUSTING

After four years the pressure had built to such an extent that my health broke down, so I nearly had to pull out of ministry altogether. I had an extended break and was able to continue, but my pattern of life and ministry was still not healthy. A few years later, after a fruitful period of ministry, I took a three-month sabbatical, which gave me an opportunity to review my life and reflect on the future. I realized that I was vulnerable physically, spiritually, morally and emotionally and that things needed to change.

I am so grateful for the lessons the Lord taught me then, which I have being trying, often feebly, to apply ever since. I now pass them on to you in the hope that they will prevent you from joining the sobering statistic of those who have had to withdraw prematurely from positions of Christian leadership. If you take them to heart, they will help you, not just to survive as a leader, but to flourish.

1. REMEMBER YOU ARE DUST

Christopher Ash twice came close to having to pull out of ministry through emotional and physical breakdown.[17] Reflecting on that experience in his book *Zeal Without Burnout*, he summarises the lessons he learnt and wants to pass onto others in five words: 'You and I are dust'. He writes: 'We need to know that and never forget it. You and I are embodied creatures: we are dust. God made us out of dust (Genesis 2:7) and one day he will turn us back into dust (Psalm 90:3)'[18]

My health collapsed in the early days of my ministry because I forgot that basic truth. I was young, I'd always been fit and well, and took it for granted that I would stay that way. As a result I pushed myself far harder than my mind and body could cope with,

---

17. Christopher Ash, writer-in-residence at Tyndale House, Cambridge, was in pastoral ministry in Cambridge, then served from 2004-2015 as Director of the Cornhill Training Course.

18. *Zeal Without Burnout*, Christopher Ash (Good Book Company, 2016) pp35-36

leaving me with chronic fatigue, headaches and anxiety.

The road to recovery began as I slowly worked out my limitations and tried to live within them. I got better at trying to find a sustainable rhythm of life and ensuring I had sufficient time for relaxation, sleep and a regular day off. I discovered what re-energized and de-energized me, and tried to ensure a balance between the two. But the most important lessons I learned went far deeper than that.

The teacher of wisdom in the book of Proverbs appeals to the younger generation: 'Above all else, guard your heart, for everything you do flows from it' (Proverbs 4:13). Yes, we must look after our bodies, but nothing is more important than the heart. In the Bible the heart stands for the control centre of our lives; it determines the convictions and desires that drive us. It was only when I recognized that behind my physical health breakdown was a spiritual heart problem that I really began to get better.

> **BEHIND MY PHYSICAL BREAKDOWN WAS A SPIRITUAL HEART PROBLEM**

I did have a genuine longing to serve Christ wholeheartedly in those early years of ministry, but, often without me realizing it, those godly passions in my heart were mixed with other misguided or sinful desires. It slowly dawned on me that I was driven as much by a concern to be thought well of and be successful as by zeal for the Lord. Perhaps there was something of a messiah complex as well – as if spiritual fruit depended on me, rather than Christ.

Looking back now, I am so grateful for the humbling I experienced in those days. At times I felt so weak that I didn't know how I would find the energy to get into the pulpit to preach. By being brought low in that way I was reminded that I can't do anything without Christ, but he can do anything without me. I am dust: God alone is God and he alone can do every spiritual work. And, wonderfully, he did work through me. I began to learn then that, far from disqualifying us in his service, our weaknesses are often the context in and through which he delights to work. As Christ said to Paul: 'My grace is sufficient for you for my power is made perfect in weakness' (2 Corinthians 12:9).

I AM DUST: GOD ALONE IS GOD

2. KEEP JESUS CENTRAL

An elderly friend, now with the Lord, rang me one morning and began by saying, 'I just wanted to talk to someone about Jesus. Do you love Jesus?'

'Yes I do,' I replied, 'but not as much as I should.'

'I love Jesus,' she said, with great emphasis. She meant it. Despite a very difficult life, her face always radiated love for him. Her example is both an inspiration and a challenge to me.

In our busyness we leaders can easily become activists, rushing from task to task, and meeting to meeting, but forgetting why we're doing it all or, rather, who we're doing it for. So it's vital we take steps to ensure the Lord Jesus remains at the centre of our thoughts and devotion.

John Newton, the converted slave trader who wrote 'Amazing Grace', chose as his personal motto: 'None but Jesus'. He longed that 'Christ may be all in all to me, that my whole dependence, love, and aim may centre in him alone',[19] but he recognized that wouldn't happen without determined effort. He wrote: 'I find that to keep my eyes simply upon Christ as my peace, and my life, is by far the hardest part of my calling... hungering and thirsting for Christ is the central daily discipline'.[20]

I can certainly echo those words. I know that my life and ministry become dry if they aren't sustained by the living water of conscious communion with Christ. And yet, perversely, I find it hard to keep coming to him to drink. The battle continues, but over the years I have built patterns and practices into my life which have helped.

Nothing is more important to me than ensuring I stick to a daily time of Bible reading and prayer. I try to keep that fresh through frequent changes: switching from longer passages to shorter ones, even just a verse or two sometimes; reading with study notes or a commentary and then without them; basing my prayers on the Lord's prayer, or another of the Bible's prayers for a while, and then writing my own, especially on significant days such as New

---

19. *Newton: On the Christian Life*, Tony Reinke (Crossway, 2015) p6

20. Ibid p17

Years Day or my birthday. I have been weak at taking a day or days for a longer time away with the Lord, but have always been richly blessed when I've done so.

And I try to remind myself to come to Christian meetings, not just as a leader, but as a disciple, so that I am feeding spiritually with others, rather than just serving up the food.

> **I TRY TO COME TO MEETINGS, NOT AS A LEADER, BUT AS A DISCIPLE**

We're all different, so we'll need to work out what helps us most to feed on Christ in those focused times with him. That will then help us walk in love and obedience to him through all of life and to keep trusting him, our sovereign Lord, whatever happens.

3. BE RUTHLESS WITH SIN

Earl Wilson was a respected pastor, but by his late forties he was living a double life and had fallen into a pattern of sexual sin. After facing up to it, seeking help and repenting, he wrote a book called *Steering Clear: Avoiding the slippery slope to moral failure*. Almost all who have gone down that slope find it hard to understand how they could have ended up doing such things. Wilson comments, 'The answer is usually found in the description of the process by which one mistake leads to another, with a disastrous cumulative effect'.[21]

We need to learn to fight sin, whether sexual or other, when it's an acorn, or else it will become an

---

21. *Steering Clear*, E D Wilson (IVP UK, 2002) p22

oak and be very hard to shift. That might begin by identifying our Achilles heels, the points of greatest vulnerability. Ask the question, 'If I were the devil, where would I direct my attack against me?' We usually know where the battle of temptation rages most fiercely when we are tired, lonely, or stressed. If we're wise, we'll make sure we give ourselves special protection in those areas. We'll need to take ourselves in hand and determine there are certain places we won't go, people we'll avoid and lines of thought we'll shut down immediately because of where they might lead.

> RESOLUTIONS ON THEIR OWN DELIVER SUPERFICIAL CHANGE

Resolutions of that kind certainly help, but I've found that on their own they will only deliver superficial change. It was a breakthrough for me when I realized that, although discipline is important, desire is fundamental. I sin because at that moment I want to. Some idol such as pleasure or popularity, has captured my heart and convinced me that chasing it, rather than obeying Christ, will give me the happiness and fulfilment I crave. But that's a lie. I know from experience that sin never delivers what it promises; in the end I always regret it. Striving for holiness in 'the new way of the Spirit' (Romans 7:6) involves asking him to expose the lies of Satan and to replace them with a deep love for Christ as well as a conviction that his ways are always best, so that I hate sin and long to walk in his ways. We're back to where we were in the last point: keeping Christ central is indispensable in fighting against sin.

I've seen some progress over the years but I still fail again and again. It's so important at those times that I don't allow shame to keep me distant from Christ, which makes it much more likely that I'll repeat the sin. I'm slowly learning not to wallow in guilt, but to pick myself up, look to Christ and once more delight in the forgiveness I've already been given through him.

4. MAINTAIN CLOSE RELATIONSHIPS

A group of us were discussing what had gone wrong after a pastor fell into sin and had to leave his ministry. 'Who were his friends?' asked someone. The silence that followed was telling.

Leaders easily become isolated. Our position sets us apart from others, so that they're more inclined to look up to us, rather than get alongside us. Some treat us as if we are on a higher spiritual plane than other Christians. One church member even said to me, 'Of course, you don't face temptations like the rest of us'. And busyness doesn't help. In the midst of all the pressures we face, it's hard to find time for family, let alone friends. But it's vital that we do. We're not meant to live the Christian life alone and, if we try to, we'll be much more vulnerable to the attacks of the evil one.

For those who are married, your spouse and your children must know that they come first under Christ. You'll need to protect your time and energy, so they get the best of you, not the dregs that are left when you've poured yourself out for others. That will mean saying no to exciting ministry opportunities and not helping as many people as deeply as you would like. But, far from undermining your Christian service, as you'll be tempted to believe, such sacrificial love of your family is fundamental to it. It will model godliness to others and will also keep you grounded. When you're tempted to believe you do belong on the pedestal others put you onto, the rough and tumble of normal family life will soon bring you down to earth. That may be humbling, but it's also healthy. True intimacy is only possible when people know us as we really are, and not just our public face.

It was sobering for me in my late thirties to ask myself the question, 'How many people really know me?' I realized I needed to make a deliberate effort to make sure that some relationships went deeper, so there were a few that were especially close. That took time and vulnerability, but it was one of the best decisions I ever made.[22]

> IT WAS ONE OF THE BEST DECISIONS I EVER MADE

I'd assumed that friendship was particularly important to me as a single man, but I soon learned that my married friends, especially those in leadership, felt isolated too. We all need those we can relax with, with whom we can share burdens, and who know both the best and the worst about us. It's been

---

22. I have written more on this theme in *True Friendship* (10 Publishing, 2013)

a great help to me to be part of an accountability group, in which we know the questions to ask of one another. That's uncomfortable, but it really helps me to fight temptation. And when I've confessed sin, they've been brilliant at pointing me again to Christ, who is the greatest friend of all.

BOILING IT DOWN

You may have noticed that all four of my points essentially boil down to one: Keep looking to Christ! In ourselves we can't keep going in Christian leadership, or even in the Christian life for a day, let alone a decade. We are very weak, but Christ is faithful and strong. With that great truth in mind, I look forward to the next 25 years if the Lord spares me, with more realism than when I began, but also with real excitement and hope.

Vaughan Roberts read law at Cambridge,[23] then theology in Oxford. He is Rector of St Ebbe's Church, Oxford, where he began his ministry in 1991 as curate with responsibility for students. Vaughan is widely used as a conference speaker, university missioner, and Bible expositor; his books have been translated into several languages. He is President of the Proclamation Trust.

---

23. Where he was President of CICCU, Cambridge Inter-Collegiate Christian Union (affiliated to UCCF/IFES).

PART II

THE SECULAR ARENA

GODLY LEADERSHIP IN THE WORKPLACE

Willy Kotiuga

Willy Kotiuga looks at ways Christian managers can bring the aroma of Christ into the workplace. His principles are transferable to all professions.

The Church teaches us to go into the whole world, but has not equipped believers with tools and with understanding of how God views the workplace. How we view work influences the way we act at work. Do we see work as a necessary evil? Do we perceive the ways we can bring influence through the work we do? For some there is an immediate link, *eg* for those working in public policy, or in product design, or as financial advisors, or for those who teach, or serve in academic administration, or in the media. But for all who serve in any roles, we can bring 'the aroma of Christ' to the way we engage with colleagues, competitors, clients and customers.

Christian believers are spread through all segments of the workplace. Some invite colleagues to join them on their faith journey. Others, while not talking about their personal faith with colleagues, allow it to shape their behaviour. The fields are ripe for harvest. In the workplace are many potential harvesters, but only a small percentage are engaged in proclaiming hope to a world looking for hope.

We are to rub in salt and shine light wherever our sphere of influence extends. This call is not only for church staff or staff in Christian agencies, but for all of us in ordinary occupations. We could be called 'the Church at large'.

> *WE ARE TO RUB IN SALT AND SHINE LIGHT WHEREVER OUR SPHERE OF INFLUENCE EXTENDS*

The call to work came in Genesis 2, before the Fall. It is good and worthy to work. Joseph's faith sustained him through four separate careers (family business, household management, prison administration, public service). Indeed it was a key in his rise to the top in each role. The Apostle Paul used his skills as a tentmaker to support his missionary endeavour, but also as a means to reaching an audience who did not engage in public discussion on faith-related matters. Daniel rose to the highest ranks, despite personal risk to his life, because of his God-given wisdom and his unswerving commitment to God's principles. For each of them, work was an offering of excellence to God.

OUR CURRENT SITUATION

Paul's tent-making inspired a generation to use their professional skills as an entry point to cultures that would be closed to 'formal' missionary work. These 'tentmaking' professionals have worked hard as civil servants, engineers, teachers *etc*. The Business as Mission (BAM) movement has taken this one step further, in encouraging and equipping entrepreneurs to set up self-sustaining businesses.[24] These businesses provide living examples of the Holy Spirit working through people, and demonstrate that honest practice works as the best business model. Biblical wisdom is always practical wisdom.

> BIBLICAL WISDOM IS ALWAYS PRACTICAL WISDOM

Throughout the world, men and women of faith meet for Bible study and fellowship before work or over lunch - in small businesses and in large corporations. These Bible studies, often open to colleagues searching for truth, help to build Christians up in their faith, and provide a means for other workers to find God. There are also nationwide associations for Christians within professions, to stimulate a biblical worldview in the discipline, and help younger members, often converted at university, to find other Christians in the profession.

Christianity is a missionary faith and the call to 'make disciples' implores us to live out that faith by inviting others to join us on our faith journey – and then by teaching them to obey everything Christ has taught us. The disconnect between Sunday and

---

24. Business as Mission is a network under the Lausanne Movement. See *lausanne.org*.

the working week has left so many people with an 'incomplete' calling.

WHERE DO WE WANT TO BE?

Imagine a work environment where there is a vibrant relevant proclamation of faith, empowered by a moving of the Holy Spirit, supported by the invigorating prayers of the local church. Do we pray for our church members as they go into the new week? Or do we tend to pray only, or mostly, for church members who are in spiritual ministry?

Rethinking 'how we do church' has become a catch phrase. Most efforts have been directed towards improving and refining existing programmes. Are there new questions to ask? There are remarkable stories of how God has been moving in churches willing to rethink how they live out the Good News.

ARE THERE NEW QUESTIONS TO ASK?

A huge potential for church growth in the next generation comes from people who hunger for meaningful relationships in the workplace. Increasingly multi-ethnic work environments in the West bring opportunity to enter into the lives of those from all nations.

We need to think more deeply about how to equip people to live and proclaim their faith at work, rather than just to be a Christian presence at work. Properly equipped, and with a holistic God-view of the workplace, workers could be highly motivated harvesters. First, the Church needs to recognize God's call into the secular professions as being a real call, as real as the call into spiritual ministry. 'The earth is the Lord's' and we need to reclaim it for him in industry, academia, medicine, the public arena...

HOW DO WE GET THERE?

There is no universal recipe, but there are key steps to moving closer to what God intends for us.

For years the church and the secular have been kept in separate spheres. In church we learn more of the Good News and how God wants to bring hope to the world. But on Monday, week after week, we offer no invitation to co-workers to discover God's grace, forgiveness and hope; it becomes 'normal' to disassociate church from work. So the gap between theology and praxis grows, and church becomes increasingly irrelevant to the workplace, while the workplace becomes irrelevant to the church.

> CHURCH BECOMES INCREASINGLY IRRELEVANT TO THE WORKPLACE

So Sunday and workweek dynamics are worlds apart, and workers and pastors live in different paradigms. Many pastors don't fully understand work dynamics. And workers have not attempted to educate pastors on the workplace. As a result, they stay in their respective worlds, meeting only at church functions. Where a worker has taken his pastor on a tour of his workplace, it has proved very enriching for the pastor and for his ministry.

Two things need to happen if the church - work divide is to be bridged: rethinking the role of the church in supporting our workplace emissaries, and rethinking the role of work in motivating emissaries.

Christian influence in the workplace can bring radical change, through the modelling of honest practice at every level, as well as through the influence of Christian thinking at a senior level. Our workplace needs to be seen as an opportunity for mission, where we can contribute Christian thinking, and bring God's love to people.

The Business as Mission movement has demonstrated that we need to be more intentional about penetrating the workplace. Its focus on the practical aspect of equipping Christian entrepreneurs to succeed should become part of the culture of the church.

> WE NEED TO BE MORE INTENTIONAL ABOUT PENETRATING THE WORKPLACE

WHAT NOW?

We have good motivational books, studies and examples – and enough guilt about not doing enough – to get a good start. What we don't have is the critical mass to build and create momentum to make the process sustainable.

Everything that we do is a gift to God, whether it is preaching, teaching, designing, cooking, cleaning, creating spreadsheets or operating a machine. All work has dignity, and all our work should reflect excellence that is a worthy offering acceptable to God.[25] We must educate church members on how to see work as their calling from God, and help clergy to see the mission possibilities in the workplace.

THE JOSEPH MODEL

Moving from where we are to where we want to be will not happen overnight. There is no magic formula, or instruction manual to guarantee results. God has blessed me with a sacred workplace where I serve him as a professional consulting engineer. I call it the 'Joseph Model' in honour of Joseph who transformed each of his work environments under adverse conditions.

We need to be committed to ongoing transformation through a daily walk with God. As we plant gospel seeds, there will be many variables outside our control, impeding growth. After years of trying to invite co-workers to join me on a faith journey, I realized that words and a personal example were not enough. Now I start the discipling process from the moment someone comes into my sphere of influence. I have the privilege of being a director of the company. This means I have responsibility to create an environment which is conducive to creating

---

25. Some churches have introduced a regular slot in the service to ask a church member, 'What will you be doing at 10 o'clock tomorrow morning?' This helps the whole congregation to get a better grasp of what it means to be the church in the world, and it expresses support for Christians in whatever the Lord has called them to do.

an excellent product and helping people attain their highest potential.

I lead a skilled group of professional engineers with projects in over 20 countries. Our primary output is high-level consulting reports for governments, international funding agencies and senior electricity company executives. The values driving our work environment include accountability, responsibility, pursuit of excellence, teamwork, discussing in a learning environment, risk-taking, forgiveness, support and celebration. These values, desirable professionally, help people embark on a faith journey. These are an integral part of making good disciples. Let's look at them:

- *Accountability* reinforces that in all areas of life we are accountable to a higher authority;

- *Responsibility* reinforces that we should work through difficulties to meet obligations and commitments;

- *The pursuit of excellence* motivates people to do better than they have done in the past and better than others are used to doing;

- *A learning environment* stimulates discussion and encourages exploration to discover more about life;

- *Risk-taking* helps staff learn to step out of their comfort zone;

- *Forgiveness* is offered to those who make mistakes or whose risks have not turned out to be successful;

- *Support* enables people to go in confidence to the next level of understanding and knowledge;

- *Celebration* is appropriate for the whole team as we share in one another's successes.

These are all Christian values and relate to the life of faith. Such an ambience provides for professional excellence and for co-workers to be discipled long before they make a commitment to faith. So when they meet Jesus and cross into a life of faith, they enter a lifestyle already somewhat familiar.

This is the sacred environment in which I live at my workplace. For others not in managerial positions, the holy ground may be limited to one's shared workspace, desk or workbench. For some, a sacred workplace is the lunchtime Bible study once a week. For others, it could be coffee breaks and/or lunchtimes filled with discussions (not monologues) about issues in life. Ultimately what transforms the secular to sacred is the presence of God – and when God is present,

> **ULTIMATELY WHAT TRANSFORMS IS THE PRESENCE OF GOD**

changes take place. We are all called to be change agents. If Joseph could do it as a slave and as a prisoner, there is no reason why we cannot transform our sphere of influence into holy ground.

The future is full of possibilities for reaching billions of workers around the world. Let's endeavour to energize, train and equip church members to practise their faith, at whatever level they serve, and to make an impact for the gospel – on the assembly line or at the head of a corporation. Let's explore ways to help workers develop leadership skills, as Christians, confident that all biblical wisdom is practical wisdom.

May God open our eyes and break down the barriers we have created so that we prepare the workplace for a faith journey.[26]

Dr Willy Kotiuga speaks widely on the value of faith in a secular environment, and actively promotes faith-based dialogue. He has over 40 years' experience of managing projects with multiple stakeholders. Willy has worked in 25 countries, advising governments on sustainable long-term strategic infrastructure planning. He was Programme Chair of the Lausanne 2019 Global Workplace Forum.

---

26. At *lausanne.org* you will find more on Business as Mission

LEADERS WHO ASK BIG QUESTIONS

Sir Fred Catherwood

Foreword to the 2007 Edition
(Light, Salt and the World of Business)

Over the past two decades there have been encouraging efforts to combat corrupt business practice, and Christian graduates have played a key role in them, personally and collectively. New movements have formed which have publicized corrupt practices, patiently resisted corrupt leaders and governments, and drawn up national and international standards and codes of conduct.[27] But there is still a huge amount to do.

As the Bible makes clear (see Genesis 6:11-12), corruption has plagued the earth ever since the Fall. It is not surprising that many people see it as inevitable, a necessary evil in the way commerce is conducted, and a means by which the rich and powerful take advantage of the poor and weak. But as this booklet shows, the Bible also makes clear that it is entirely wrong, and it calls us to take a stand against it.

As individuals, we may feel helpless victims of a system that we cannot change. Worse, we may have

---

[27]. For example Transparency International's *Business Principles for countering Bribery*.

become complacent about it. Worse still, in today's materialistic culture, we may have been seduced by it. Corruption is globally endemic. It is not confined just to a few countries, or just to poor ones.

Corruption is not only morally wrong. It undermines economic development, distorts fair decision-making and destroys social cohesion. It is dishonouring to God and the antithesis of showing love to our neighbour.

Sir Fred Catherwood draws on a lifetime of experience in business and public service. In this distinctive piece he shows how each of us can bring change to our nation by aiding the fight against corruption. I hope it will prompt and stir discussion and action right around the world.

Paul A Batchelor
[Then] International Advisory Council, Transparency International; Chairman, Crown Agents

Sir Fred Catherwood writes for young professionals in business or industry. As well as managing their teams and meeting goals, they could take a broader, global, perspective – and ask how they can help bring change. Again the principles have parallels in all professions. ⟶

LEADERS WHO ASK BIG QUESTIONS

From *Light, Salt and the World of Business*

Sir Fred Catherwood

HOW HONESTY CAN HELP TRANSFORM NATIONS

The most notorious bribe in history is in the Bible. It is the thirty pieces of silver given by the Jewish priests to Judas Iscariot, to lead them to the Garden of Gethsemane, the overnight resting place of Jesus and the other apostles. There Judas showed them by a traitor's kiss which of the figures in the dusk was Jesus. For Judas, money meant a lot more than loyalty or love. He was motivated by greed and personal gain. When he realized with horror the consequences of his betrayal, he threw the money into the temple and committed suicide.

BRIBERY IS CONDEMNED THROUGHOUT THE BIBLE

Samuel was the first of the Old Testament prophets and a great leader of Israel. But when he grew old, he appointed sons in his place who 'did not walk in his ways. They turned aside after dishonest gain and accepted bribes and perverted justice' (1 Samuel 8:3). The perversion of justice is one of the worst consequences of bribery, enabling the rich to exploit the poor. In his farewell address to his people at the coronation of King Saul, Samuel said, 'From whose hand have I taken a bribe to make me shut my eyes? (1 Samuel 12:3). He had been blameless and the crowd declared without hesitating: 'You have not taken anything from anyone's hand.'

King David of Israel raises a rhetorical question in Psalm 24 'Who may ascend the hill of the Lord? Who may stand in his holy place`? He then answers the question himself in the next verse: 'He who has clean hands and a pure heart, who does not lift up his soul to an idol or swear by what is false'. In Psalm 26 as he prays for vindication, he sets in contrast men 'whose right hands are full of bribes' and the man 'who does not take a bribe against the innocent' (Psalm 15:5). Israel's great prophet Isaiah commends the one 'who keeps his hand from accepting bribes (Isaiah 33:15) and the prophet Amos laments, 'You oppress the righteous and take bribes and you deprive the poor of justice in the courts' (Amos 5:12).

In the first century AD Paul the Apostle refused to bribe the Roman Governor Felix. The Governor admitted Paul had done nothing wrong, but he kept him in prison 'because he was hoping that Paul would offer him a bribe' (Acts 24:26). This time could have been spent in visiting and encouraging

PAUL REFUSED TO BRIBE THE ROMAN GOVERNOR

the churches he founded, or in making his intended evangelistic visit to Spain. But no, he would not pay this sum which he could easily have raised from a rich Christian. No excuse for bribery could be greater than that faced by the Apostle Paul, and he refused to make it. Instead of visiting the churches, he had to write the letters to them which still guide the churches today. Our suffering for the sake of the gospel is not lost in God's providence.

These passages show that in both Old and New Testaments, bribery is regarded as a sin against God; a perversion of justice which allows the rich to exploit the poor, and an abuse or exploitation of power to satisfy greed. They teach that the people of God must be honest. And I commend a careful study of Joseph, and, centuries later, of Daniel. In each case, it was their consistent integrity that won over the trust of the nation's leader, who rewarded them with significant authority.

> *CONSISTENT INTEGRITY WON THE TRUST OF THE NATION'S LEADER*

SOCIETY DEPENDS ON TRUST

Society depends not only on personal honesty (like honest insurance claims and the honest paying of taxes), but also on public honesty. By contrast, bribery and corruption damage the fabric of a country, they risk political stability, and they discourage economic development.

One example of public honesty is the conferring of university degrees – the honest judgment of university professors that those to whom they have given degrees will have the knowledge and skill to cure the sick, or to make our aircraft safe. It stands to reason that no-one can trust a profession in which its workers gain qualifications by bribing their trainers or professors. For the economy to work at national and local levels, the professions need to provide good service at an agreed cost. This is critical, as every country depends on the integrity of its skilled professions, which form the heart of industrial society. Here we see the interconnected nature of student life and the national economy; industry depends on the integrity of the university.

> INDUSTRY DEPENDS ON THE INTEGRITY OF THE UNIVERSITY

Many people persuade themselves that, since bribery is the custom in their country, a bribe is excusable. It is a way of speeding up matters, or giving a little extra to underpaid officials. This last reason is dangerous. It masquerades as compassion but silently approves a system where receiving a bribe has become necessary for anyone wanting to earn a decent living.

While serving as chief executive of companies operating in international trade, I saw that corruption not only undermines a country, but that it is bad for business. Singapore has no natural resources, yet its tough anti-corruption laws and severe penalties from its post-war new beginnings, have made it one of the richest countries in the world. Like Singapore, Japan has put all its energy into industrial development and attempted to set a climate for ethical business.

South Korea has a similar story. These are attractive countries for investment. No-one wants to invest in a country which lacks effective procedures against corruption.

There is a clear correlation between low levels of corruption and successful business. Successful business needs trust between buyer and seller. This trust relies on assurance that the product being exchanged will be up to standard, delivered on time, with loans repaid and workers receiving their due wages.

JOSEPHS AND DANIELS

The Josephs and Daniels of our time need to be committed for the long haul. Prof Jerry Ghana, who served under five Nigerian Presidents – Christian and Muslim – made public service his life's work. 'I am asking God to give me fifty years,' he said. 'The political situation in Nigeria cannot be changed overnight.' Jerry Ghana became a Christian through Scripture Union in Nigeria, and his faith was nurtured in his student years in Ahmado Bello University, Nigeria, and then Aberdeen University, Scotland. What enabled him to stand firm?

First, he had learned through Scripture Union and NIFES to abide in Christ by observing the lives of the staffworkers. He had sought to walk with the Lord each day, meditating on Scripture and cultivating a disciplined spirit of prayer.

Secondly, he had chosen his friends and his partnerships carefully, as reputations can easily be damaged by association. Other Nigerian politicians had been derailed through associating with those who were to prove themselves corrupt. He said he learned this lesson from the way Daniel chose his friends.

Thirdly, he realized the importance of legacy. He believed that the political landscape could be changed in Nigeria through Christian influence. The evangelical Clapham sect in London had helped to bring about the abolition of slavery in the early 19th century. Wilberforce and Shaftesbury were a model for future generations of Christians in politics.

THE PROTESTANT ETHIC

A study of the Reformation in Europe is key to understanding our culture today. Having the Bible in the common language of the people broke the monopoly of the bishops (appointed by monarchs) in determining what people were taught about their faith. As people learned to read, they could see what was biblical and what was not. When monarchs gave patronage rights to certain individuals and made them rich, and those people in turn oppressed the poor, Christian believers protested, basing their protests on what they knew from scripture. This led to a growing nervousness among the monarchs and bishops, and one by one the Reformers were exiled. When the Reformer John Knox returned to his native

Scotland, he travelled back via Geneva, the self-governing Swiss reformed city-state. The values he encountered in Geneva gave him ideas; he used these ideas to instigate reforms in Scotland which were to be far-reaching.

Europe's post-Reformation Calvinist churches gave a good model for public life. They created a counter culture from which emerged the early 'Protestant ethic' of innovation, hard work and mutual trust. This resulted in financial independence for the Protestant churches from the culture of corruption around them. The Protestant ethic in daily life developed trust between buyer and seller, lender and borrower. It produced a vigorous trade between the Protestant countries of Switzerland, the Netherlands, Scotland, England, New England and Prussia.

REFORMS IN SCOTLAND WERE TO BE FAR-REACHING

The Protestant ethic is based on Christ's teaching that we should work to multiply our talents, behave ethically, and not be extravagant in lifestyle. See the parable of the talents in Matthew 25:14-30 and a similar parable in Luke 19, which underline the message. We learn that whatever your gifts or talents, you should invest them so they yield returns. These two parables help young professionals better understand the world of industry and commerce. This ethical living led to the accumulation of capital which paid for the trading ships and laid the basis for trade expansion and technical development for economic prosperity.

The Protestant Reformation created change in church life and in ways of thinking. Protestant churches no longer focused on expensive edifices and extravagant worship. They emphasized instead personal relationship with God, fellowship with other believers, and caring for our neighbour. In their spirituality, there was no longer a divide between secular and spiritual. The faith of the believer affected all of life, which included the use of God-given skills for productive work. This ethic developed into what the historian Herbert Butterfield described as 'a shuttle of ideas between the English, the French and the Dutch'. Out of this grew the 'scientific method' of enquiry.[28]

To a final year student looking for a job in a culture of bribery and corruption, the Protestant ethic may seem no more than a distant vison, or ancient history. One Christian student said to me despairingly, 'Where do we begin?' I trust he and many in this generation will find help and strengthened resolve in these pages.

THE RISE OF SELF-REGULATING PROFESSIONS

The major goal of professional life can be described in three ways: (i) to develop and add to the body of

---

28. An agreed approach for (a) investigation, (b) acquiring new knowledge, and (c) correcting and integrating previous knowledge. It is based on gathering observable, empirical evidence which is measurable, and which is subject to recognized principles of learning.

knowledge through research; (ii) to provide services for the public and private sectors of society; (iii) to train the next generation, and pass on accumulated knowledge. The professions maintain their standards through regular examinations, and their discipline though actions against those who infringe or violate professional codes of conduct.

Over time professions diversified into different fields. For example the engineering profession separated into the related yet discrete fields of electrical, mechanical, civil and aeronautical engineering. As the professions started to form, a new discipline of accountancy became recognized in its own right, with the development of the limited liability company and trading in shares. It is a discipline which is necessary to preserve the framework of the rule of law and the maintenance of public trust.

ONE GRADUATE TAKES A STAND

A young engineer from South Asia joined his father's electronics business. In their culture, extra payments to officials were the custom, and his father duly paid them. This young man was torn between his Christian convictions and loyalty to his father, and struggled to know how to respond. He eventually concluded that he should try to persuade his father to split the business. He would focus on export, choosing markets where he need not bribe. Within a short time, his sales were fifty percent greater than his father's.

In countries with a culture of autocracy and oligarchy, bribery and corruption often flourish, and young graduates cannot look to the government for help. So how can they break free of the cycle? How can they trade ethically? Most won't find themselves in the position of our South Asian friend. They have to find other ways out of the old culture.

The high tech industry has become an open field to invest and grow a business. It is possible to develop a company from scratch on the internet, with little capital and without a plant or staff; a huge number of entrepreneurs are doing this. Christian graduates in materially-privileged cultures would have more reason than others to explore these possibilities. The Apostle Paul urged the richer churches to help the poorer, and this principle of helping God's people is no less appropriate in business. If Christians in the West sourced their goods only from those who trade ethically, these markets would flourish.

THE POTENTIAL FOR CHANGE

In many countries, Christian graduates find themselves in senior positions in the public and private sectors. With the spread of Christian student movements, the proportion of Christian graduates globally has risen rapidly. More than in previous generations, they have greater opportunity to see themselves in an international context and to discuss issues with fellow Christian graduates from other countries. While church and mission leaders can discuss these matters, it is the professionals themselves – doctors, engineers, scientists, lawyers and business managers – who are most keenly affected by the gulf between Christian values and the values of their culture. They are also the ones who can drive change.

> **THEY ARE THE ONES WHO CAN DRIVE CHANGE**

The fight against dishonesty has to be a wholehearted effort by the entire church, and not left as a battle to be fought only by those who live in overtly corrupt cultures. This united declaration would gain broad public support from all well-thinking people who dislike the practice and who see how it ultimately undermines and damages any society.

Christians are 'the salt of the earth' and the prime purpose of salt is to prevent corruption.

It is very hard for a Christian to be effective alone, like one solitary grain of salt. Christians owe it to their country and to God to get together with fellow professionals, and to strengthen each other's hearts, minds and arms. The writer to the Hebrews urged believers to strengthen their 'weak knees'.

I once met a brilliant young Christian doctor from Central Asia who refused to work in his country's hospitals. Hospital care was supposed to be free to every citizen, but nurses and doctors had to be bribed to provide care and treatment for patients. He could not see how he could change that system. The rapidly-growing national church did not want to jeopardize religious freedom by appearing to oppose the government. He saw the problem as entrenched, and in his frustration planned to emigrate. The story of this young graduate is typical of so many whose professions place them at the heart of their country's economic and political life. They have to work out their obligation to Christ and to the culture in which they live. Like Isaiah, they may have to say 'I live among a people of unclean lips...but...'

On a visit to Kenya, my wife found a low-tech group of countrywomen dedicated to encouraging small farming. It seemed a tough job, but the women had no time for those who were always seeing problems and finding excuses, rather than trying to solve the problem of poverty. They believed in honest work, though hard work, to get them out of poverty.

> **THEY BELIEVED IN HONEST WORK ... TO GET THEM OUT OF POVERTY**

Over the years, meeting students in different places has left vivid impressions in my memory. I remember a gathering of Christian students in Eastern Europe in a seminar on bribery and corruption. The room was crammed. The subject seemed to be a problem which was tearing them asunder. I remember one girl weeping. She had passed her finals, but the Professor would not recommend her for her award until a 'favour was granted'. What should she do? The alternative was to repeat her course for another year, despite the cost to her family who were already making sacrifices for her study. As she said, 'They usually don't dare to turn you down twice.'[29]

A year later I remember an even bigger meeting on the same subject. The students seemed depressed. 'Where can we begin?' they asked. The easiest answer (for those with financial means) was to emigrate to the West. But this would not serve their country, to which they felt an allegiance, and in which their families would remain. It would not shake the salt which they were supremely well-placed to shake.

Christian mentors in senior professional roles need to devise ways for young graduates to use their God-given gifts to transform their own culture and society.

WHERE DO WE GO FROM HERE?

Rich countries with a strong church pour great effort and energy into aid for countries with a fraction of the income of the West. The awful poverty of the 'two-thirds world' is highly visible. It wrings our hearts and we want to do something, anything, which relieves poverty and suffering. Who would not? But whatever we do from the outside will not, indeed cannot build an honest indigenous infrastructure. That can be done only from inside.

---

29. In several countries in Africa and in Latin America, it is common for male students to pay a bribe and for women students to be asked for sexual favours in return for exam passes. Corruption in all such universities has reached a new low, and is undermining the fabric of these nations. Where there is a high incidence of STDs, this abuse of women could wreak deep agony for families for many years to come. It is wonderful to see the courage of Christian students who will not pay these bribes.

In human terms the university is the most influential institution in any country. To renew the university will transform the society. While Christians in academia work towards that high goal, Christian graduates can be active on a wider front, in shaking salt into their professions.[30]

Through networking with Christians in business from other countries, I believe many new entrepreneurs could succeed in the same way as the graduate in South Asia found success, by choosing export markets where they need not bribe. It would not be easy, but I believe it would be possible. Imagine what could be achieved through Christian graduates in countries with minimal corruption (no country is free of corruption) opening up markets for fellow Christians in corrupt countries, matching up buyers and sellers? To coordinate this would be a full-time job for skilled merchants in international trade. I believe it could be done.

> *TO RENEW THE UNIVERSITY WILL TRANSFORM SOCIETY*

Movements like IFES, Navigators, Cru, Youth for Christ, OM and Lausanne have worldwide networks of Christian graduates. Their potential to equip Christian students at the undergraduate level, or to equip Christian professionals globally is second to none. How can we exploit these potentially formidable global networks?

---

30. Agencies help people find faculty positions, short- and long-term, in universities around the world. Some countries require a higher degree.

Some time ago the General Secretary of the British IFES movement (UCCF) brought together a group of graduates in senior positions in industry. The agenda was to look at the Christian's contribution to industrial society. Now it would extend to the technology industry in particular. IFES publishing houses have produced titles in these areas and we need more for each generation – a steady flow to keep a bright vision for the fragrance of Christ in business life, in the development of technology, and in political life.

NETWORKS

Many Christian graduates work in the public sector: in local government, medicine, education, tax administration, and so on. Some work in policy formation and administration, in key positions of influence, and also positions of great temptation. Christians in the public sector need prayerful support from their churches and Christian associations. A strong national network could make a significant mark on a culture of bribery and corruption. Beyond that, to be part of an international network of Christian professionals, giving mutual support, and focused on making a difference in their cultures, would be a great source of strength.

The Lausanne Movement networks provide fertile soil for meeting with like-minded people, and possible future business associates; fellow graduates who want to shake salt through the practice of ethical dealings. From here groups of friends can naturally form: friends in industry, politics and academia, both within continents and across continents. Let us not underestimate what informal networks could do nationally and globally. But neither must we underestimate what Christians are already contributing.

> **LET US NOT UNDERESTIMATE WHAT INFORMAL NETWORKS COULD DO**

LAUNCHING NEW PRIVATE SECTOR BUSINESSES

As we have seen, there is unprecedented opportunity to create new private sector businesses, and to increase international trade online. Christians in cultures of greater corruption might begin by focusing on export markets, dealing only with those whose business practice is honest. The Business as Mission network, which sprung from Lausanne, has seen many new endeavours and we need more.

I close with two examples, one from the former Soviet country of Moldova and the other from Rwanda. Over the decade following the collapse of Communism, Moldova's economy shrank by seventy percent; corruption was endemic; and unemployment was a feature of life, with eighty percent of the population living below the poverty line. The government was thus starved of tax revenue and the infrastructure was crumbling.

Norman Fraser, a graduate of UCCF UK, saw the need to resuscitate Moldova's industry, to model honest practice, and to create jobs for graduates, while at the same time nurturing the skills of the country's wider work force. As a result, Brains Direct was founded in 2000 by Norman with three Moldovan partners. Within five years the company had nearly 200 staff, all fairly paid and all paying taxes. In 2006 it merged with a London-based IT consulting and services organization to form Endava, drawing on the best talent from the West and from emerging Europe. Its blended sourcing created a highly-skilled cost-effective operation with delivery centres in Moldova, Romania and the UK, servicing clients across Europe and the USA. Endeva was recognized in the prestigious 2009 Deloitte Technology Fast 50 award programme.

At a Tedx event in December 2013 in Whitehorse, Yukon, Norman Fraser reflected on Brains Direct, and on the questions he urged his staff to ask. What did they hope? He helped them to think creatively in order to unleash imagination; to dare be counter-intuitive; to suspend their disbelief. It would be a small goal simply to become the best IT company in a country which had no other.

Great leaps forward, he said, have often emerged where creatively-dissatisfied people push beyond easy notions of success. Weakness should be identified, so it can be turned into opportunity. In a weak economy, such as was their context, a company can work cross-border, selling into strong economies while paying its own staff well. This in turn enables it to create more jobs. He urged his staff in Moldova to think of success not as being the best, but, albeit counter-intuitively, as being a company where some of the best people leave to start rival companies. After ten years, the IT industry in Moldova contributed ten percent of the country's GDP.

The hundred-day Rwandan genocide in 1994 left nearly a million dead. No family was left untouched, and many of the workforce were orphaned or dealing with deep trauma. In the years following the genocide, thousands of students listened to Bible teaching, as they saw the gospel offered hope, though they themselves were not committed Christians.

At a meeting in 2003 arranged by the Christian Union in the National University in Butare, three Christian visionaries discussed an idea.[31] Could they form a consultancy which was run on Christian principles, offering training and financial services as a means of influencing business practice? Could this become 'an engine of sustainable change' in the nation? It was a big dream. The International Business Center (IBC) began in 2006 with one staff member, one laptop, and six months' lease on a one-room office.

> IT BEGAN WITH ONE STAFF MEMBER

By 2008 there were nine part-time staff and five offices. The IBC was not set up to offer jobs, but to help people to create their own, and to do so in a way which would truly benefit society. Graduates of other student movements looked to the model with a view to beginning parallel initiatives. The IBC

---

31. Anicet Munyehirwe, Mudenge Theophile and Juvenal Hategekimana

founders drew up a Memorandum of Understanding that one percent of all profits would be given to the Union des Groupes Bibliques du Rwanda (IFES) as a means of supporting the ongoing ministry which was so formative for them. A further ten percent of profits generated by the movement's graduates serving on staff would be given in addition. They clearly saw the need for a healthy ministry among students, to feed more Christians into the workplace.

The following year, one of the founders, Anicet Munyehirwe, wrote, 'When we started, people didn't believe that this new system of entrepreneurship without funds would work. We began only with new graduates, and no project like it had existed before. But after three years, we proved that it can work.'

His report demonstrated the confidence of clients and of an increasing number of partners; the IBC was now working with non-governmental organizations (NGOs) like CARE International, SNV, Netherlands development organization and USAID as well as with the Rwandan government and the police. The young staff were clearly gaining significant experience.

NO PROJECT LIKE IT HAD EXISTED BEFORE

Bee-keeping is traditional in Rwanda. It is well-served for this through its natural resources of forest and eucalyptus plantations, and bees need only low-cost investment. The Directors of IBC sensed there was further room for expansion, so they founded a new company, the Rwanda Beekeeping Company (RBC

Ltd). Through the RBC they are working to expand the capacity of production by setting up local co-operatives. Within their first year they had trained 179 families in the techniques of beekeeping and raised them out of poverty, with a total harvest of three tonnes of honey to sell.

IBC was soon supporting coffee farmers, again creating co-operatives and opening up markets. These co-operatives also create roles for field workers, accountants and translators, drawn from among the Christian graduates. To encourage more new graduates to launch out in other African countries, they have arranged workshops on entrepreneurship, and they now act as consultants for capacity building.

ALL THE RAW MATERIAL IS HERE

At the most profound level, few would dispute that honest practice is best, but it takes courage to believe it from within the culture, when success, or plain survival, seem to depend on quick gains.

Will we see a new generation of leaders showing the caliber of the biblical examples of Joseph, David or Daniel? Could we see a whole new wave of business enterprise like that of the Hugenots or the Quakers? Let us spur one another on in the business world. Our nations are crying out for honesty and courage.

> *NATIONS ARE CRYING OUT FOR HONESTY AND COURAGE*

My prayer is that this will strengthen the nerve of new graduates in the world of business. We have all the raw talent to succeed, and our global network is formidable. May God keep the prophet Micah's words (Micah 6:8) in the forefront of our minds as we consider our own career paths, or indeed advise others entering these arenas, whether in private enterprise or public service. And may the Lord prosper the work of our hands, and of our emails, and of our conference calls, for his glory.

Sir Fred Catherwood (1925-2014), an industrialist with wide experience in the political arena, chaired several senior bodies, including the National Economic Development Council ('Neddy') and the British Overseas Trade Board. He entered politics in 1979 as a Member of the European Parliament, becoming its Vice Chair from 1989. Sir Fred was a founding father with Klaus Schwab of the World Economic Forum ('Davos'). For more, see his entry in the Oxford Dictionary of National Biography.

IDEAS FOR REFLECTION AND DISCUSSION

PART I: LEADERSHIP IN CHRISTIAN MINISTRY
With transferable material for leaders in the secular workplace

IF I AM TO LEAD D E HOSTE
This is divided into 14 sections. You could cover a section per week in a study group, drawing out the main points of each paragraph. Hoste's writing is rich and purposeful, and there is much which could be explored. Some in the group will bring experience of where the principles outlined have been put to the test. Younger leaders will be able to ask questions. As Sinclair Ferguson said in his Foreword, he wished he had read Hoste's wisdom long ago.

FIVE MARKS OF A CHRISTIAN LEADER JOHN STOTT
You could take each of these five marks and discuss them. While there is overlap with Hoste, Stott comes in from a different angle. A useful question for this section could be how to nurture each of these five in emerging leaders.

THE LEADER AS SERVANT AJITH FERNANDO
Again, each section lends itself to careful study. Perhaps friends could commit themselves to reading it on their own first, with prayer, and letting scripture

search them. Then gather together to look as a group at what it may mean to lay down our lives; to have a 'theology of groaning'; to yearn for others; to share our lives as the Apostle Paul did. How can and should we avoid unbiblical stress? How can we preserve our joy in the Lord, and keep spiritually fresh? How can we gain strength from the Lord to help us withstand blows? What unchanging truths motivate us? Becoming disillusioned will depress us, and make effective ministry impossible. How can we help one another not to become disillusioned, but to stay strong?

LEADERS WHO LAST VAUGHAN ROBERTS
This is a critical chapter for all in ministry. Its four sections could be covered separately, or you could look at the whole chapter if you have 90 minutes. If you go for this option, ask everyone to read it carefully on their own before you discuss it. How does it affect our ministry to remember that we are dust? How can we keep Jesus central in our varied pressures of life and work? There are significant practical applications to be talked about, for example: rhythms in ministry, handling sin, and cultivating friendships. Perhaps you could agree to look at this again with your group in six months' time or in a year's time.

PART II: LEADERSHIP IN THE SECULAR WORKPLACE
Will aid understanding for those
in spiritual ministry

GODLY LEADERSHIP AT WORK WILLY KOTIUGA
Willy Kotiuga is an engineer in a global company.
If there are managers in your group, ask them
first to explain their context to the group. Do they
feel supported by Christian friends? How can the
church support them better / understand more
of their pressures? How can the 'Joseph Model'
be transferred? Is it a good working model? Are
there professional groups of Christians which your
members could usefully join?

LEADERS WHO ASK BIG QUESTIONS
FRED CATHERWOOD
This chapter, different in kind, has several aspects. It
takes a bird's-eye view of a nation and its professions,
with an historical sweep. It assumes that Christians
will want to see corruption dealt with. Then it reaches
for practical solutions and tells some deeply-inspiring
stories. There may be entrepreneurial sixteen-
eighteen-year-olds, as well as students and young
professionals, who could have their imagination fired
by some of these ideas.

For managers: what would it look like for you to
lift your eyes from the management of your team,
and your immediate goals? Could you find Christian
partners in a culture of corruption, and open a market

for them? Could you build a business in a weak economy to help create wealth in that economy, and model honest practice?

Are there others to whom you could give or lend a copy of this book, who would find a particular chapter helpful?

APPENDIX 1

SOURCES

If I am to lead. *D E Hoste*. Collection by Alan M Stibbs of correspondence in Phyllis Thompson's biography *D E Hoste: A Prince with God* (CIM 1947). First published as a collection by CIM/OMF 1968. Reprinted several times by CIM/OMF and IVF/UCCF to 1981. Completely revised for easier reading by the current editor, and published as *36 Steps to Christian Leadership* (OMF International, 1999). The 1999 version is used here.[32]

Five marks of Christian leadership. *John Stott*. Based on several sources, including personal conversations, John Stott's preaching, and friends' reminiscences; together with *Issues Facing Christians Today* Chapter 17 entitled 'A call for Christian leadership' (Zondervan, 1982; then HarperCollins, updated by Roy McCloughry).[33]

The leader as servant. *Ajith Fernando*. Address to the annual conference of the Evangelical Missionary Alliance (now Global Connections) at High Leigh,

---

32. See the short biography *Live to be Forgotten* by Patrick Fung (OMF Hong Kong, 2008. Third edition, 2013.)

33. Also see *Calling Christian Leaders* (IVP). For those who would like to read more widely: all John Stott's books are easily found, and many sermons are archived on *allsouls.org*

Herts, UK, 1997. First published by OMF International 1999. Reprinted 2001 with a Foreword by David Pickard (available on dictumpress.com). Revised and expanded edition published by IFES/OMF International, 2006; then as a Didasko File, 2008. Also known to have been published in print in Nigeria (English); Korea (Korean); Hong Kong (Cantonese); Thailand (Thai); Brazil (Portuguese); and in South Asia (in Marathi, Kannada, Hindi, Tamil and Sinhalise).

Leaders who last. *Vaughan Roberts.* Plenary address to the Lausanne Younger Leaders' Gathering, Jakarta, Indonesia, July 2016. Video available at *lausanne.org*.

Godly leadership in the workplace. *Willy Kotiuga.* Multiplex address given at the Third Lausanne Congress: Cape Town 2010. First published in the official record of the Congress: *Christ our Reconciler: Gospel / Church / World* (IVP-UK and IVP-US, both 2012).

Leaders who ask big questions. *Fred Catherwood.* Excerpts from *Light, Salt and the World of Business* (first published by IFES, 2007; then as a Didasko File (2008. Reprinted 2009. Revised 2012. Reprinted 2013). Also known to have been published in print in Ghana and Nigeria (English); Brazil (Portuguese); Hong Kong (Cantonese); and India (Marathi, Tamil).

TRANSLATION RIGHTS AND EXTANT TRANSLATIONS OF SECTIONS

If you (i) wish to explore translation rights for this book; or (ii) have questions about extant translations of sections as listed above; or (iii) know of further English-language editions or translations not listed, please contact the Editor through *dictumpress.com*.

APPENDIX 2

THE ART OF GOOD GOVERNANCE

In a book on spiritual leadership, it seems appropriate to include a note on governance. We hope that what follows will be of help for those who serve as CEOs or as Board members of mission agencies, seminaries, or Christian publishing houses. There will be transferable principles for church leaders and church Councils. It is intended as a checklist, rather than a handbook.

This Appendix assumes that Board members understand the legal requirements of charity Trustees as laid out by their government, and that they are conversant with the body's constitution or Memorandum and Articles. It also assumes that the body has in place a doctrinal basis,[1] and a clear document on vision and values.

---

1. The doctrinal basis will serve as the movement's anchor. It may be borrowed from another ministry. For example many inter-denominational ministries have adopted the doctrinal basis of the IFES movement in their country, or the Cape Town Confession of Faith. The doctrinal basis should be seen as a 'minimum' and a 'maximum'. If a person cannot gladly adhere to each part, we have to conclude that that person is not an evangelical; and if a person wants to add an additional clause, he or she is requiring more than the ministry, or scripture, requires. Ministry staff of many bodies signify their adherence to the doctrinal basis each year, by signing it.

INTRODUCTION

History has shown that good governance can assure success in the outcomes of the work; and conversely, where governance is weak, the whole ministry will be weakened and its future effectiveness can be put at risk.

Members of a governing body are the Trustees of that ministry, and as this name implies, are entrusted with its life. They carry responsibility for passing the ministry on to the next generation, effective in its calling, and in a spiritually-healthy state.[2] An invitation to serve on a Board is not to be taken lightly; nor indeed to be regarded as a means of conferring status. While carrying significant responsibility, it is, as the verb conveys, a way of serving.[3]

A Christian's first priority will naturally be the local church. Alongside the local church, it is not possible to serve more than a handful of other ministries well. An invitation to join a Board may need to be declined, in order to serve more fully on other fronts.[4] For the Board to function well between meetings, its members must be able to do more than be present each time it meets.

---

2. Some ministries or institutions may have a Board and a separate body of Trustees. In these cases, the Board is no less responsible for keeping the ministry aligned, so for simplicity, the term 'Board' here refers to both levels of governance.

3. The UK Charity Commission offers helpful publications available free online, such as document CC3; its second chapter outlines the duties of Trustees.

4. While there can be no hard-and-fast rule, some ministries will ask that Board members place their ministry no lower down than third in terms of priority.

✔ 1. ROLE AND PURPOSE OF AN EFFECTIVE BOARD

The Board guards the vision and strategic direction of the organization / ministry. It oversees the ministry through the CEO, who in turn works with his/her senior team. The Board is responsible for ensuring (i) the ministry's continuing strategic alignment with its purpose and values; (ii) its ongoing financial viability and financial good conduct; (iii) its theological integrity; and (iv) its statutory compliance, such as annual reports to the Charity Commission, Companies House or other regulators.

It is important to distinguish between 'governance' (the role of the Board), and 'management' (delegated by the Board to the CEO and senior staff). It is sometimes said that the most important decision of the Board is to appoint the right person as CEO (or, in the case of a local church, as church leader). But this does not minimize the role of the Board at all times.

Principles, policy and practice: The Board ensures that the *principles* of the organization, especially its 'objects', are followed correctly; and that the CEO maintains the principles and the objectives / purpose of the organization / ministry, which do not change. Matters of *policy* require careful discussion and are not changed lightly.[5] Areas of *practice*, which must keep changing to retain effectiveness, will be

---

5. Changes of policy would normally be agreed by the Board. Depending on the matter in question, it may be helpful to draw in Board members for consultation as discussions progress.

delegated to the CEO as he / she works within the strategic direction set by the Board.

✔ 2. PROFILE OF AN EFFECTIVE BOARD

An effective Board for any spiritual enterprise will include members with specialist backgrounds, as outlined below. There are four essential marks common to all Board members, namely to:

(i) be in full accord with the doctrinal basis of the movement / institution, and with its mission;
(ii) understand, and endorse, the need for this ministry in its wider context;
(iii) have, or work to build up, a grasp of the ministry's history and values; and
(iv) demonstrate in their own lives a desire to grow in the knowledge and love of God.

As vacancies arise, the selection process for finding new Board members may require wide consultation. Typically, a nominations committee is appointed by the Board to search for candidates and propose them for final interview and election by the Board. In some cases, especially in older charities, the election is conducted by a wider body of members or similar officers depending on the original constitution.

In most charities the chair is either elected within the Board by the existing Board members, or directly *appointed* by the Board after an external search; either way it is a good idea to agree from the start that, if possible, the chair will serve for at least two successive terms in the interests of stability.

If Board membership is limited to people the current Board members already know, the ministry may be missing out on the best people. Often there can be a wrong assumption that the current leaders know all the best people. Some Board members will be 'home-grown', that is former staff of the mission agency or graduates of the student ministry, but each should be invited on the strength of the specialism or specific facet of wisdom and experience he or she brings. Every Board needs at least one member with financial competence. That member is often given the role of Board Treasurer. Where an additional Board position can be filled by someone who also has a good understanding of financial matters, this is to be welcomed, but is not essential.

Facets of wisdom and experience: An increasing raft of policies and protocols is required by governments for bodies claiming charitable status. These include, for example, policies on: workplace safety; safeguarding of children and vulnerable adults; the proper handling of donations, and giving to external bodies. Further, such protocols and policies include important clauses on people with disabilities, on ethnic diversity, and on matters of sexuality. Many of these will require an understanding of employment law, and of how to make a case for exemption, where that is appropriate / possible.

Each of the following four facets is important in governing a ministry, to ensure the ministry's effectiveness, and to meet fiduciary responsibilities and associated legal accountability of the Board.

(i) theological understanding;
(ii) a grasp of current trends in the area in which the movement or ministry is engaged; and a knowledge of trends in society as they relate to the mission of the movement;[6]
(iii) deep experience in financial matters and fund development;[7] and an understanding of how to identify and manage the risks to which the ministry is exposed and to which its operations are susceptible;
(iv) familiarity with employment law.[8]

---

6. This pairing of trends (in ministry and in society) will encompass sociological and philosophical, as well as theological and missiological.

7. A clear understanding of financial matters is vital for financial planning. This does not require a major donor to be placed on a Board because of that person's means. All members, regardless of personal means, must be selected on the strength of their grasp of the mission or ministry. Some missions have used Chris Wright and John Stott's *Money and the Gospel* (Dictum / EFAC, 2019) in approaching donors.

8. This does not require having a Board member who is professionally qualified in this area. But the Board and CEO should identify a qualified person whom the CEO or HR manager could consult informally for advice and support; or formally for paid advocacy, if needed. In a ministry context, HR issues can require not only technical knowledge, but spiritual wisdom. Related to this: It will be important for the CEO to ensure a clear grievance procedure is in place, so staff know they will be listened to, and that they have recourse to an appeal process, in line with Matthew 18:15-18. This spiritual wisdom will avert much difficulty. It should not be used on its own, however, if, in rare cases, outside authorities should be informed, eg if illegal practice has taken place.

Where a Board has grown without careful strategy, it can be useful to have an audit of members' skills to identify any area of deep experience which is missing. If aspects of understanding are lacking, the ministry will be weakened or jeopardized.

There may be testing times when together the Board will have to work to discern the way forward. Based on a sense of the ministry's history and values, and each of the above facets of wisdom and experience, the Board will play the role of the 'men of Issachar': those who understood the times, and who knew what to do.[9][10]

There have been sad stories of Boards which have lacked in one or more area, or have sat loose to their history or values, or have been over-zealous in drawing in younger and therefore inexperienced members.[11] No Board is immune from becoming weakened, and the Board Chair must remain vigilant. The Chair needs to be watchful for voices on the Board and in senior management that are too

---

9. See 1 Chronicles 12:32

10. Each new appointment to the Board is important to get right. As names arise, they will be discussed by the whole Board, and the CEO's comments sought before a final decision is reached. Approaches should not be made informally by a Board member to 'sound a person out'. This can create embarrassment if the Board decides not to invite the person; or can make the Board feel under pressure to do so. All approaches must come only on the authority of the Board after open discussion. Some Boards invite potential members first to become participant-observers in one or two meetings before they commit themselves.

11. On younger leaders: some agencies invite them initially onto regional councils or special interest committees. A strategy to invest in able, committed, younger people, who learn the values and culture of the movement, will be invaluable for the ministry for decades to come.

dominant, at the expense of quieter voices being heard.

✓ 3. ORIENTATION OF NEW BOARD MEMBERS

New members can familiarize themselves with recent Minutes, but that is not sufficient orientation. While Board members each bring different specialisms, all need to become conversant with the past history of the movement, and the reason for its values. Only with this combination of history and values can a Board calibrate ideas. Together with the senior leaders, they then work towards a future vision, which is kept aligned with the original vision and purpose. kept aligned with the original vision and purpose.

✓ 4. GUARDING THEOLOGICAL INTEGRITY AND FINANCIAL INTEGRITY

Formal structures need to be established to guard the theological integrity and the financial integrity of any ministry.

Theological integrity: The Board may appoint a theological adviser, or theological working group, to be chaired by a Board member. A small ministry may approach a larger trusted ministry to ask if their theological advisers may be willing to suggest names who would help in this capacity. Well-intentioned initiatives without deep biblical reflection could veer a movement gradually and imperceptibly off-course. The theological integrity of all aspects of ministry and publishing will be maintained only with constant vigilance. This underlines the place of the doctrinal basis as an *anchor*. To change the metaphor, it also acts as a *flag* around which staff and supporters rally. Some ministries take time to work through the doctrinal basis with all levels of leadership, from Board to small groups, to ensure that: (i) its tenets, and (ii) its dual roles of *anchor* and *flag*, are owned and understood.

Financial integrity: This extends to donor recruitment and development, to all budgeting for ministry expenditure, staff salaries and pensions, and to investment and accounting.[12] These matters could be handled by a finance / business advisory group chaired, for example, by the Treasurer on behalf of the Board. The CEO would normally be a member of this group. The Treasurer would then bring proposals to the Board.[13]

The Board's responsibility in accepting a budget is based on its understanding of the figures presented.[14] The Board as a whole will bring insight and foresight. It is critical for the Board to be fully informed on financial matters, and for no information

---

12. See *Money and the Gospel* for biblical insight on financial integrity.

13. This group's remit should include: (i) understanding the provenance of all donations and other income, and whether such gifts and income are given with any restrictions or 'strings attached'; and (ii) ensuring that appropriate internal controls are in place within the ministry, including segregation of duties, to ensure that cash and other assets are protected from risks such as theft, fraud and unauthorized expenditure.

14. Some Board members, who are less familiar with accounts, may need more explanation so they can participate in the discussion.

to be withheld. Lack of information can lead to uninformed judgment and cause irretrievable harm to a ministry. Accounts must be audited in compliance with Charity law.[15]

☑ 5. THE CEO'S ROLE IN RELATION TO THE MINISTRY, AND TO THE BOARD

The CEO is responsible for vision casting, and for the overall management of the ministry. This will include the appointment of senior staff.

Checks and balances are important. Many organizations have a rule that the appointments of all leaders of departments or functions will be confirmed by the Board. While Board members with particular interests or specialisms may be drawn into the interview process for senior appointments in an advisory capacity, it is good for the CEO to make the final decision, subject to the Board's formal confirmation.

The CEO will work closely with the Board Chair, who will often become the CEO's first-line confidante. It is vital: (i) that a Board Chair has capacity and ready availability for this commitment; and (ii) that each have a high level of trust in, and respect for, the other.

---

15. In some situations the recommendations of an auditor can usefully be shared with the wider support base, to alert them to important financial developments.

It is good practice for the CEO to be entitled to attend each of the Board's sub-committees or working groups.

The CEO will often act as Secretary to the Board. Board members need to be well-informed, with regular reports, and well-prepared papers for meetings, including, as above, a clear set of accounts. Ideally, Minutes of all meetings, agreed for distribution by the Chair,[16] should be sent out within two weeks at most, to ensure timely action on matters while the meeting is still fresh in people's minds.

Reporting and Appraisal of the CEO: The CEO will report to the Board through its Chair. The Chair will ensure that the CEO is appraised at least on an annual basis, often with a mid-year review, to ensure his/her effectiveness in the role. There is no single pattern for this, and sometimes in larger organizations, three or four Board members would meet with the CEO for an unhurried session, and work through major strands of the ministry – their state; their challenges; and the CEO's leadership of them, personally and through the senior team.

This appraisal should not be seen as threatening, but as an expression of partnership. It is a means of confirming that: (i) the Board and the staff continue to share a common vision, and (ii) the CEO is proving effective as a leader. It also provides opportunity to

---

16. The Minutes will be amended, if necessary, and then agreed formally in the following meeting, but it is important for what essentially remains a draft to be agreed with the Chair before distribution.

ensure that the CEO is adequately provided for, and that his/her family is not facing hardship.

Opportunities for the whole Board and the senior team to meet each other can strengthen a sense of trust and partnership. Such gatherings will also help the Board to understand more of the ministry dynamics and any strains, and to know of pressures felt.[17] It is good practice to invite leaders of ministries / functions to be present at Board meetings where the Board will discuss matters which relate to their area, so they and the Board can hear each other's insights.

Appointment of a new CEO: The Board will typically determine the job description and profile for the CEO, then the Nominations Committee will start to receive suggestions of names, and to search for candidates who (i) fit the profile and (ii) demonstrate the necessary experience. As with the appointing of new Board members, work will be needed to ensure that the best person is found, as he or she may not already be known to the Board.[18] From the search, the Nominations Committee, in consultation with

---

17. In addition to meeting senior staff, it can be good for Board members to meet staff at all levels, if there is opportunity, both to offer encouragement and to keep their finger on the pulse. In conversation with staff, Board members must be mindful that the Board operates only as a whole body; and individual members should avoid giving any wrong impression that they speak for the Board, or carry any personal authority. Board authority is exercised only in meetings which are quorate, and where members vote on issues, on the strength of informed discussion.

18. To reach this stage, some Boards will employ a trusted search agency.

the Board Chair, will ideally nominate two or three candidates for an interview process.

It is unwise for the Board Chair and the CEO of a charity or ministry to be members of the same family. Greater accountability is required than this relationship could afford. Should the Board appoint a CEO who is a close friend of the Chair, a wise Chair will stand down and hand over his/her office. For a close friendship in this context, even with the best of intentions on both sides, could similarly impede objective appraisal of the CEO and his / her leadership. Further, this would leave the staff feeling vulnerable as they would now not be able to appeal past their CEO with any confidence, if need were to arise.[19]

The chosen candidate will demonstrate proven ability (i) to work under authority; (ii) to delegate confidently; and (iii) to work with staff who have greater gifts in some areas. Each area can be explored in interview.[20]

There is no 'pass' or 'fail' in the appointment procedure. We believe that the Lord creates the good works for us to do. While most new CEOs will meet

---

19. While it is rare, and a serious step to have to appeal past a CEO, such a course of action may become necessary, as a last resort, and provision needs to be there for it.

20. The CEO works under the authority of the Board with confidence. That is, grasping the partnership between them in pursuing the goals of the organization / movement. The Board's direction and setting of strategy is a means of enabling a CEO, not a means of policing. The interviewing procedure should probe past experience: how a person dealt with real situations in previous roles. 'What would you do if...' questions are to be avoided. Instead ask: 'Tell us of a time when... What did you do?'

a majority of the prescribed skills and abilities, any remaining gaps can usually be filled either by further training or by redistribution of tasks. In any case, at the interview stage there is always an option not to appoint any of the candidates, and to extend the search process.[21]

✓ 6. BOARD PROTOCOL

Handling major issues: As Board decisions by their nature will have long-term impact, they should not be rushed. Major issues can be brought to the Board (with supporting papers) for preliminary discussion, with a view to more discussion at the following meeting, before a vote is taken. It may take further thought, prayer, consultation, fact-finding, before a decision can be reached. Discussion in meetings is best-handled through the Chair at all times, and conflicting views can then be heard, calibrated, and where necessary mediated.

Cycle of business: The Board Secretary will ensure an annual cycle of business, so all aspects of the work across the calendar year are overseen. The Chairman and Secretary can work to facilitate a periodic self-review of the Board in terms of its effective leadership and its development. This can sometimes take the form of a residential overnight meeting.

---

21. Psychometric testing may be worth considering as part of a second interview for senior staff, or for the selection of new Board members. It can confirm strengths and weaknesses while potentially highlighting an area which conventional interviewing could miss.

Conflicts of interest: Conflicts of interest for any Agenda item need to be declared at the start of the meeting. These may be obvious, or more nuanced. For example, where *pro bono* work from Board members' friends is to be welcomed, care must be taken that this not be rewarded in less-tangible ways, for example permission to use the charity's name to seek further voluntary sector clients. In addition, it is good practice for all Trustees to declare all conflicts of interest annually; these can then be assessed for their materiality and any appropriate action taken, should problems be envisaged.

 7. SUPPORTING THE BOARD

The Secretary will work closely with the Chair in preparing Agendas and Minutes for Board meetings. The Agenda should include accompanying papers which give Board members the information they need to prepare for the meeting. Judgments are only ever as good as the information on which they are based. The Agenda will ideally be sent out at least two weeks in advance to allow time for Board members to read it unhurriedly, and pray. If there are major issues they wish to raise at the meeting, this also gives a chance for them to contact the Chair or Secretary in advance, to alert them.

The Secretary will be responsible for agreeing the Minutes with the Chair before they are sent out; and then for tracking the action points to ensure each is addressed. Careful Minutes are vital, not only as a means for tracking action points, but also in creating the historical archive of the ministry. Further, they will inform future discussions, so the movement can learn from its history. Physical sets of Minutes should be indexed, and bound every five years, together with appropriate accompanying papers. Archive libraries will require such physical copies for future historians, alongside a digital archive, transferred as needed over time to successive new forms of storage.[22]

We trust this checklist will prove useful. Contexts vary, and adjustments may be needed. While written for a ministry context, there are transferable principles for secular charities. Spiritual wisdom, as mentioned earlier in the book by some writers, is always practical wisdom.

Compiled by the Editor in consultation with senior leaders and Board members from several ministries.

An expanded version of The Art of Good Governance is available in booklet form, in multiples of 5 and 10 copies, for distribution to members of Boards, Trusts and Councils. Published by Dictum in association with Premier, with a Foreword by Charles Clayton.
ISBN 978-1-8380972-5-7

---

22. For clarity in the historical record, it is best practice for members to be referred to with a full Christian name or more than one initial, rather than a single initial: Peter or Petra Smith or P Y Smith, rather than simply P Smith.

WHO WE ARE

Dictum was founded in 2018, and is based in Oxford. It publishes books for the West and the Global South which are biblical, pastoral and incisive. Dictum's lists (see over) include classic reprints. Churches or agencies ordering in bulk, perhaps for a special event or anniversary, are invited to add their logo and a description of their ministry at the front of titles purchased. Review copies are available at no charge. For more, visit *dictumpress.com*

The Evangelical Fellowship in the Anglican Communion (EFAC) was founded with prescience in 1961 by John Stott. EFAC works to enable Anglican leaders around the world to stand firm, to engage thoughtfully with secular trends, and to articulate a persuasive biblical response to them. Its Theology Resource Network (TRN) draws senior theologians from all continents. The Church of England Evangelical Council (CEEC) is its affiliated group in England. To learn more, and to view their publications, visit *efacglobal.com* and *ceec.info*

'Clarity and brevity are two great gifts to the world.'

Dictum's books do not waste words, or waste the reader's time. They bring biblical thinking which is refreshing, clear and well-applied.

Dictum has four lists:

Dictum essentials: Core books for wide use in churches and mission agencies, with questions for personal reflection or discussion.

Oxbridge: Church history from the ancient university towns of Oxford and Cambridge. Including a Reformation Walking Tour; and a humorous feline view of Oxford.

Unique angles on John Stott's ministry, including the remarkable story of Frances Whitehead, his secretary for 55 years, a story which needs to be preserved; and a fun authorized children's biography.

List Four: A growing and diverse wider list of pithy books, longer and shorter.

dictumpress.com
books worth reading more than once